Tillsonburg Ontario in Colour Photos, Saving Our History One Photo at a Time

Photography
by Barbara Raué
2014

Series Name:
Cruising Ontario

Book 81: Tillsonburg

Cover photo: 38 Ridout Street West

Series Name: Cruising Ontario
Saving Our History One Photo at a Time

Tillsonburg is a town in Oxford County located about fifty kilometers southeast of London on Highway 3 at the junction of Highway 19 which connects to Highway 401.

The area was settled in 1825 by George Tillson and other immigrants from Massachusetts. A forge and sawmill were erected and roads built which led to the establishment of a settlement on the Big Otter Creek originally called Dereham Forge.

In 1836 the village was renamed Tillsonburg in honor of its founder. It was also in this year that the main street, Broadway, was laid out to its full 100-foot (30 meter) width. Because the village was predominantly a logging and wood product center, the street width was to accommodate the turning of three-team logging wagons. This width has become a benefit toward handling the pressures of modern-day traffic by providing angled parking. The extension of Broadway north was called Plank Line and is now known as Highway 19.

The water system supplied pure water for domestic use, and provided water power to such industries as a sawmill, planing mill, grist mill, spinning mill, pottery and a tannery. Many of these new establishments were owned, started, or financed by George Tillson.

In 1915, a Public Library was built with funds provided by the Carnegie Foundation, and the town's Memorial Hospital was constructed in 1925. In the 1920s, major enterprises included milk production, manufacture of shoes, tractors, textiles and tobacco.

Table of Contents

Tillsonburg

Tillsonburg

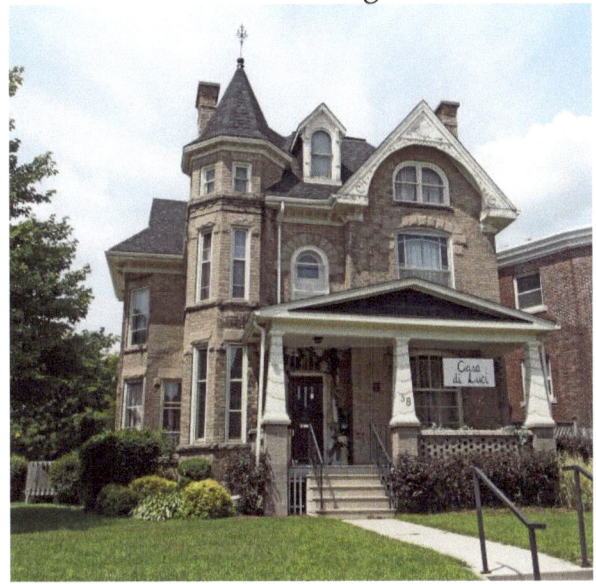

38 Ridout Street West - Casa di Luca Restaurant
Queen Anne style, vergeboard trim on gable, turret

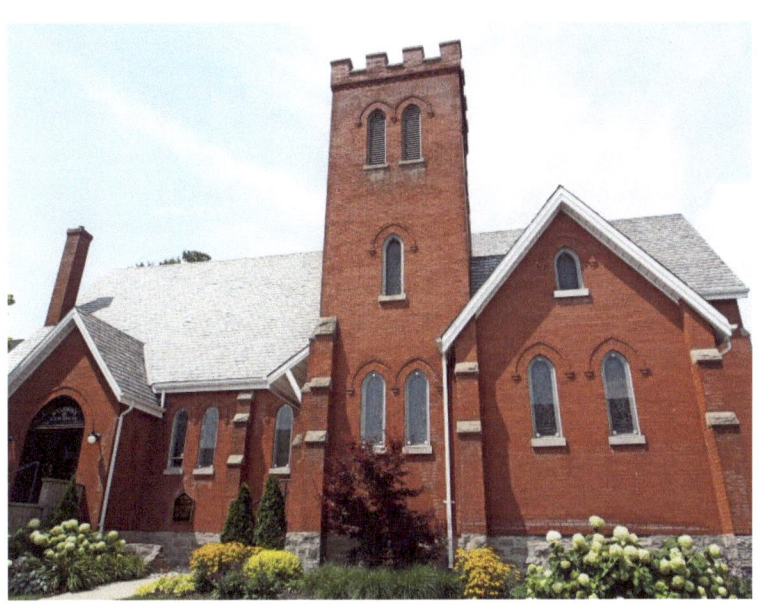

46 Ridout Street West – St. John's Anglican Church A.D. 1899
– Gothic Revival - Lancet windows, buttresses, battlement

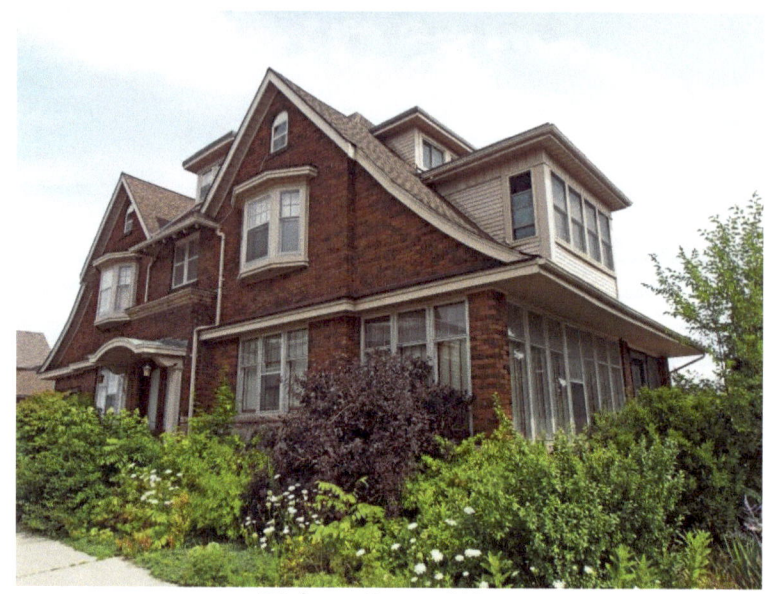

Ridout Street West

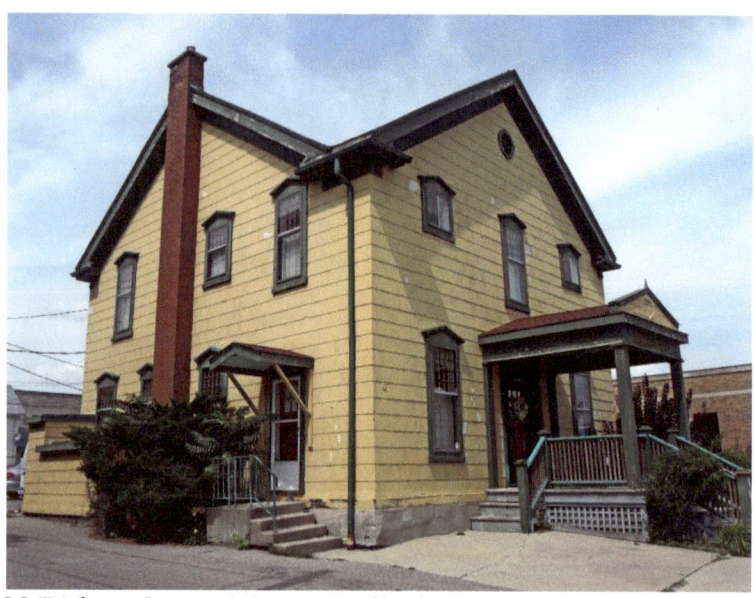

20 Ridout Street West – Pedlar's Quay – Gothic Revival

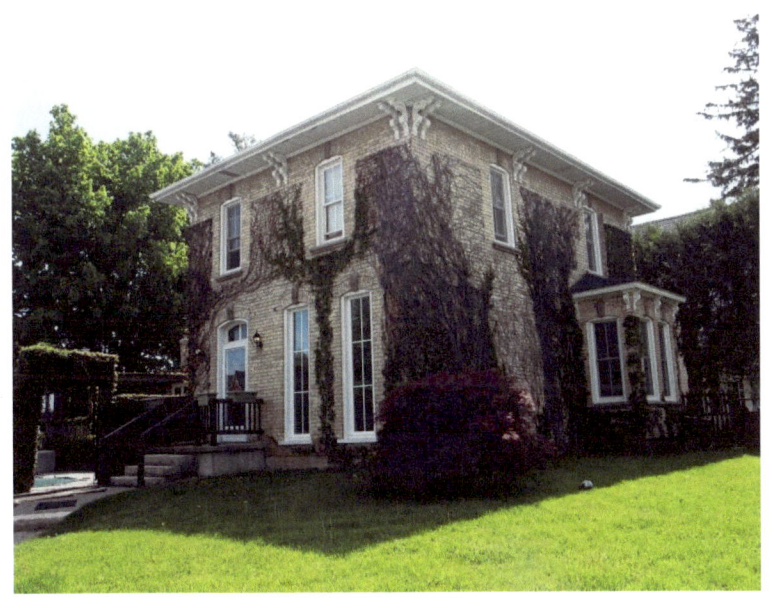

59 Ridout Street – Italianate – paired cornice brackets, bay window, voussoirs and keystones, transom window

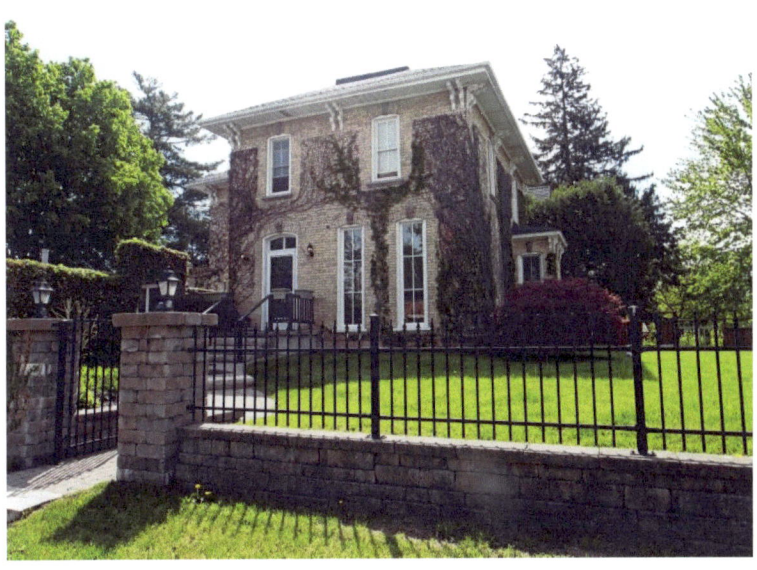

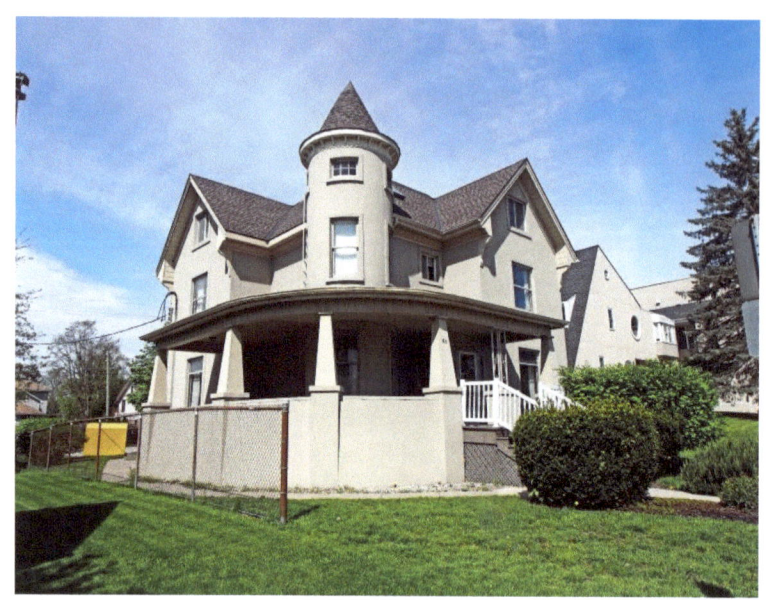

65 Bidwell Street – Queen Anne – turret, wraparound veranda

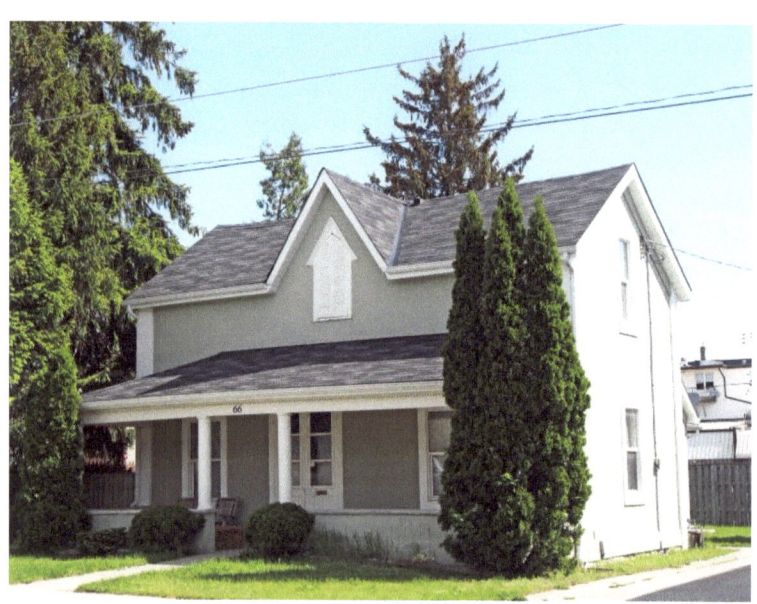

66 Bidwell Street - Gothic

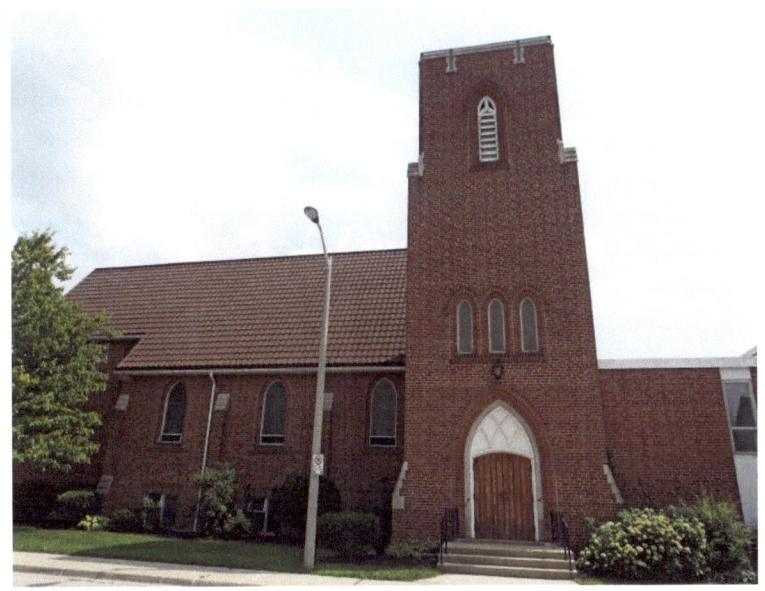

101 Bidwell Street – First Baptist Church

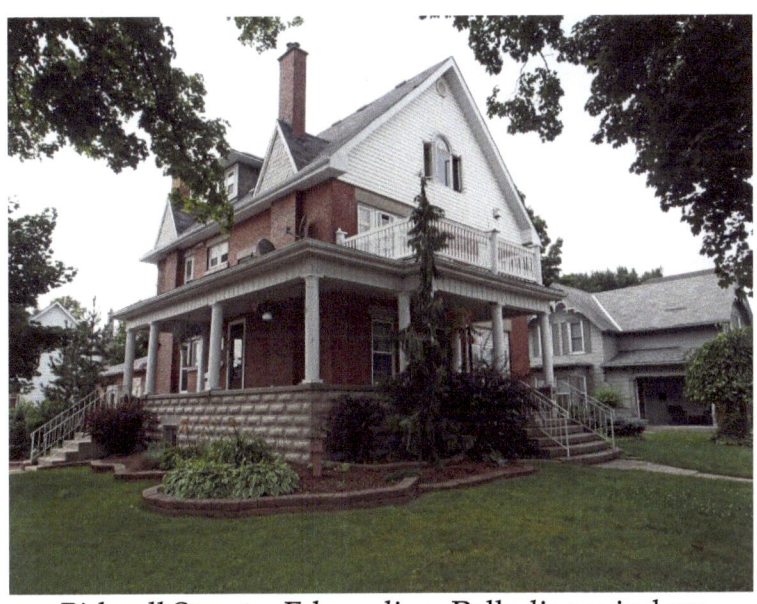

Bidwell Street – Edwardian, Palladian window

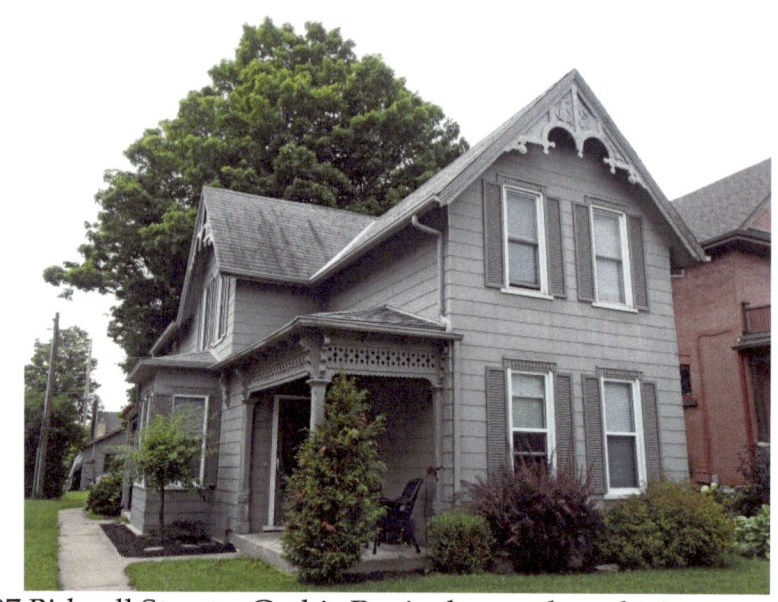

107 Bidwell Street – Gothic Revival, vergeboard trim on gable

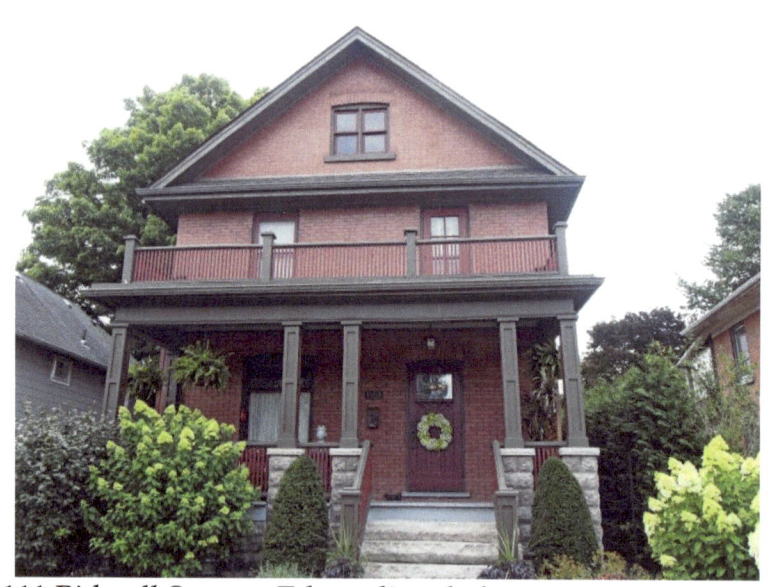

111 Bidwell Street – Edwardian, balcony on second floor

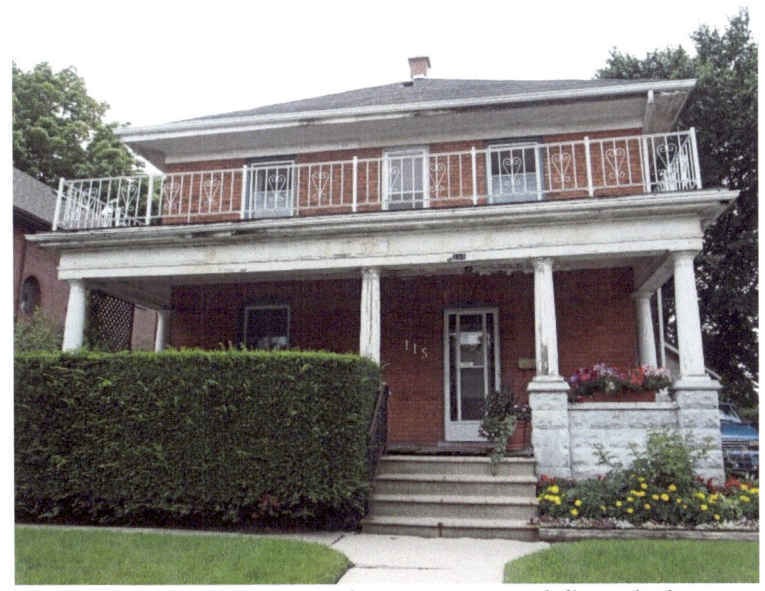

115 Bidwell Street – Italianate, second floor balcony

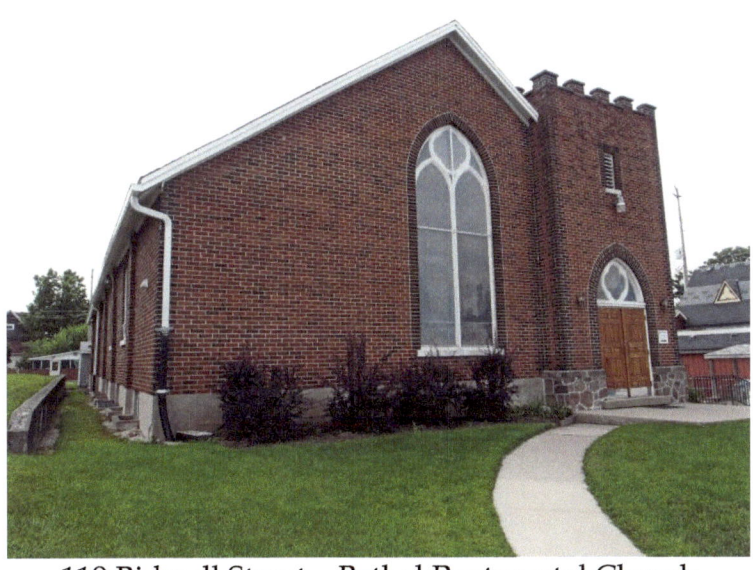

119 Bidwell Street – Bethel Pentecostal Church

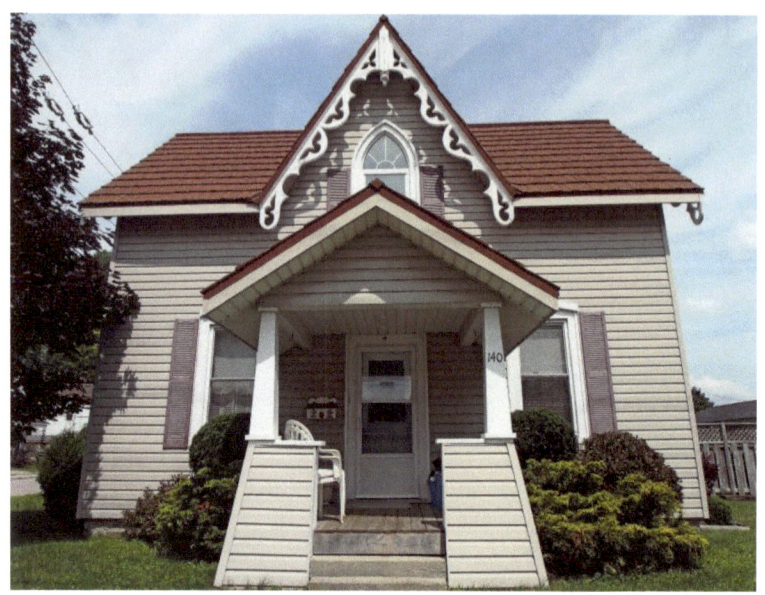

140 Bidwell Street – Gothic Revival, vergeboard trim and finial

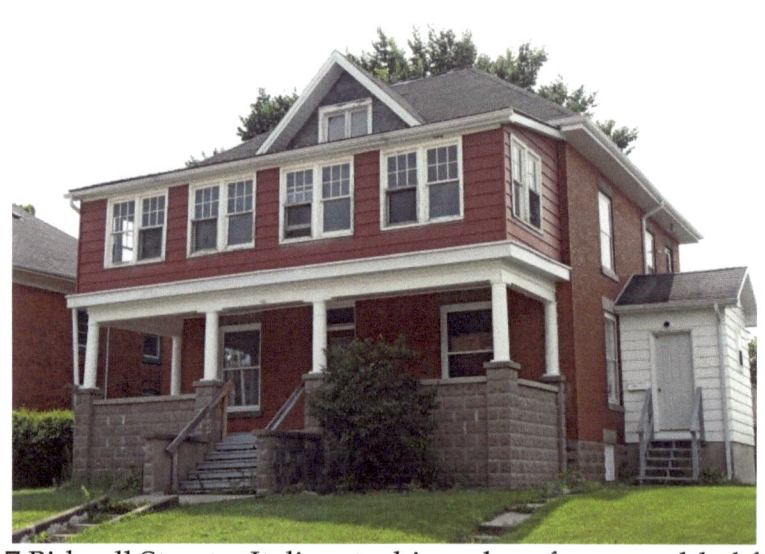

117 Bidwell Street – Italianate, hipped roof, room added full width of the house above the veranda

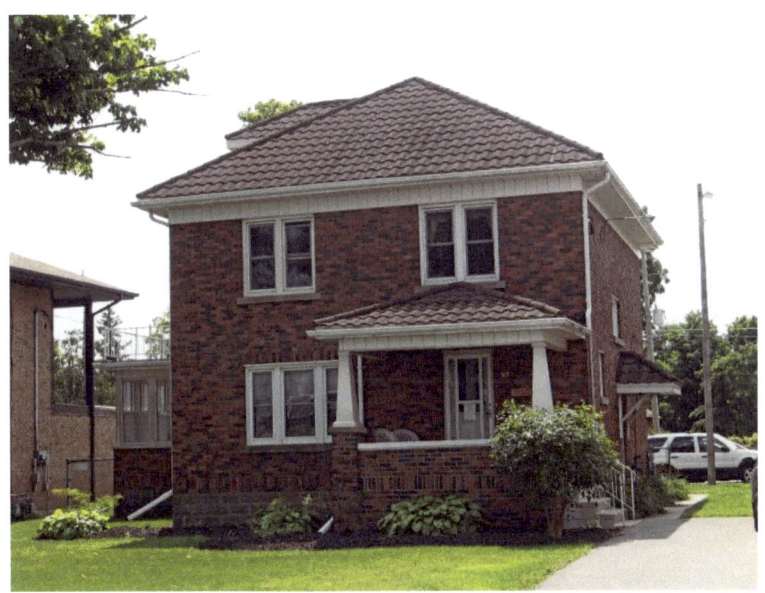

97 Bidwell Street – Italianate, hipped roof

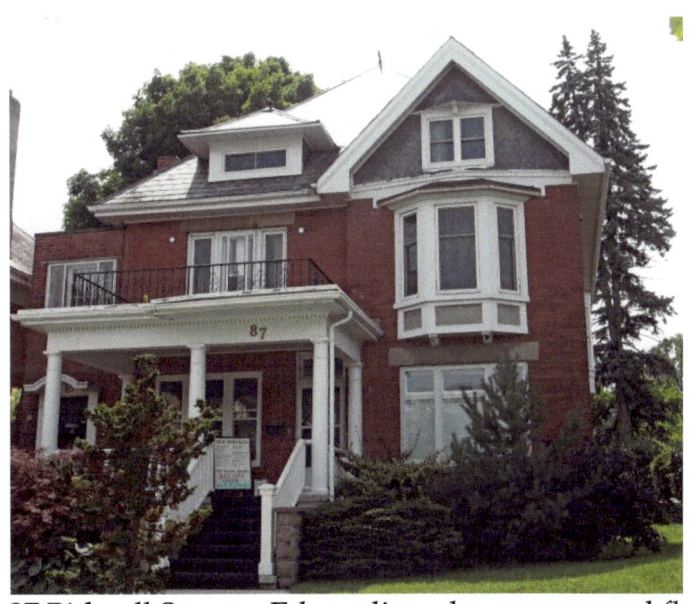

85-87 Bidwell Street – Edwardian, dormer, second floor balcony, second floor bay window

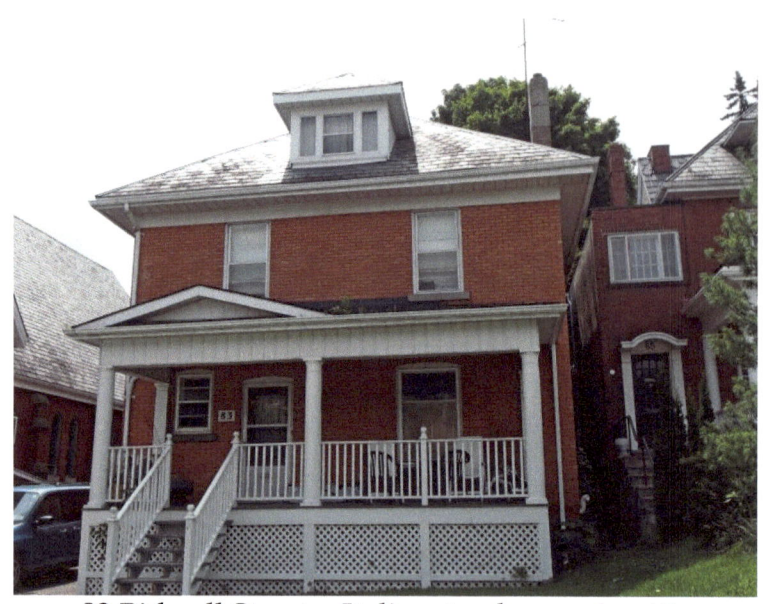

83 Bidwell Street – Italianate, dormer in attic

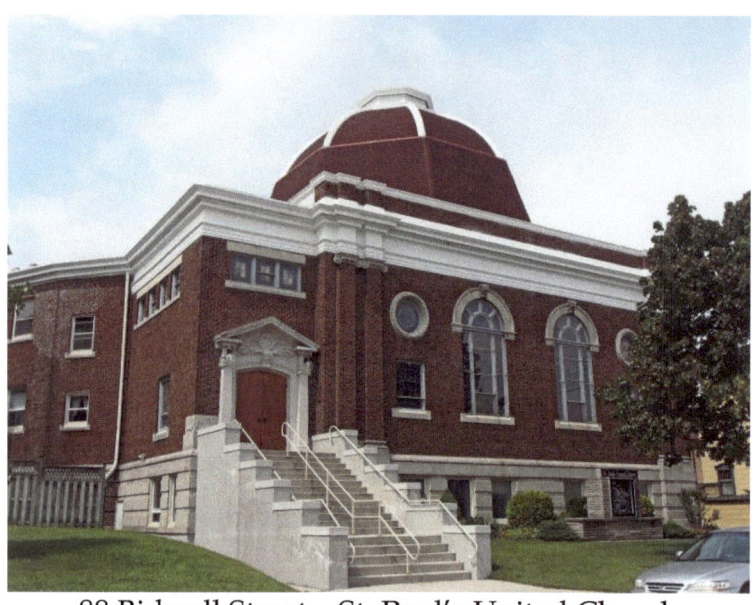

88 Bidwell Street – St. Paul's United Church

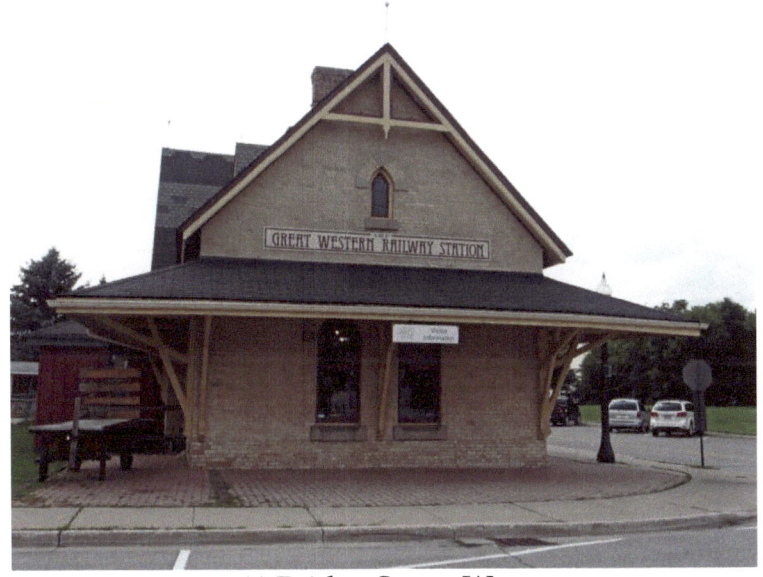

41 Bridge Street West

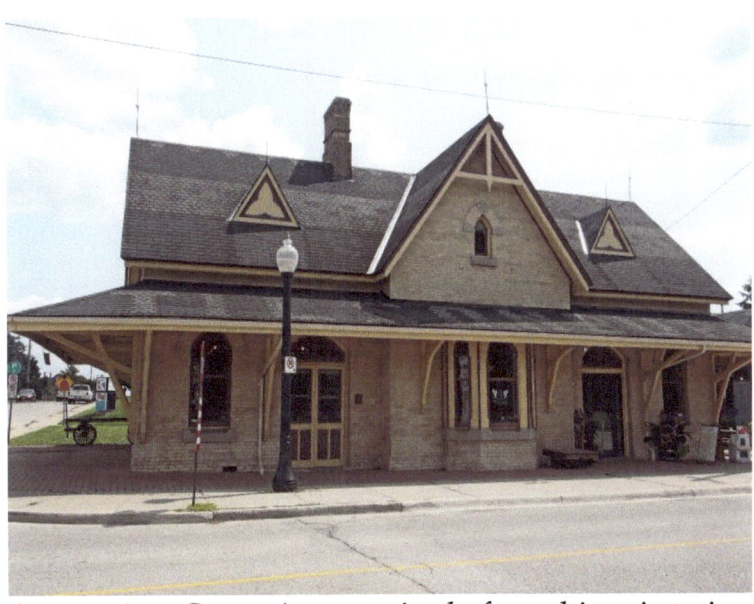

The Station Arts Centre is comprised of two historic train stations. The Great Western Railway Station was built in 1879 and is located on its original site.

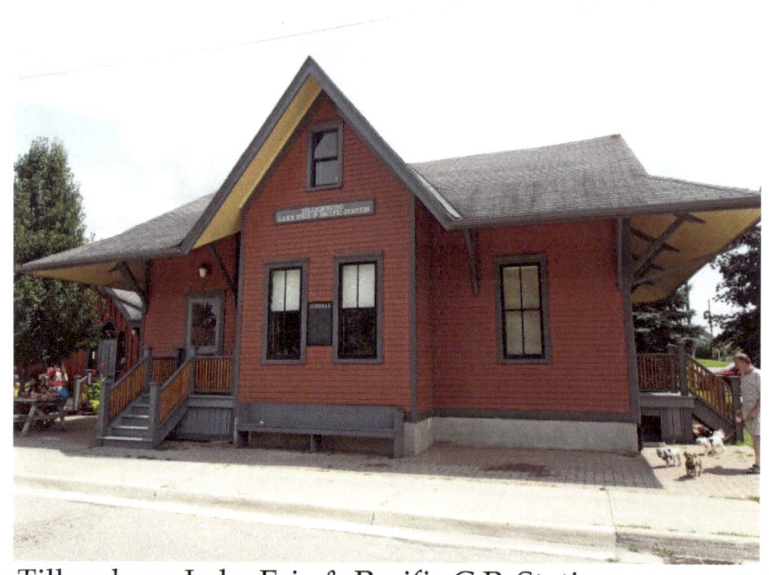

The Tillsonburg Lake Erie & Pacific C.P. Station was moved to an adjacent property in 1994 from its original location on King Street.

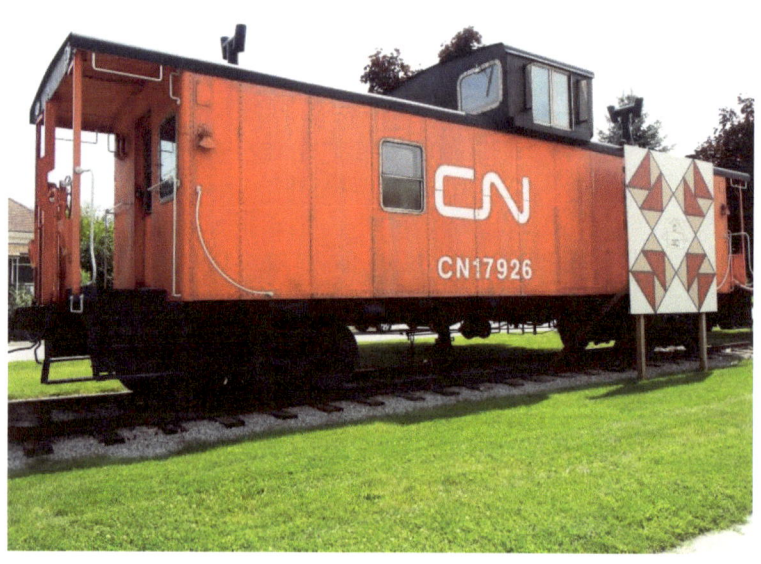

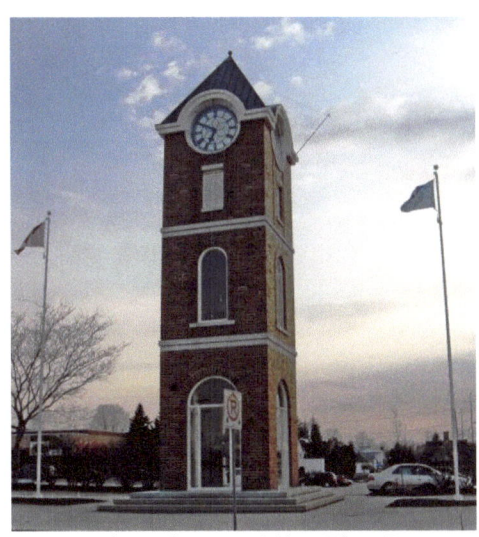

41 Bridge Street West (Highway 19) - The Rotary Clock Tower is located at the corner of Bridge and Broadway Streets. The clock came from the old Post Office, and the bell from the old Town Hall.

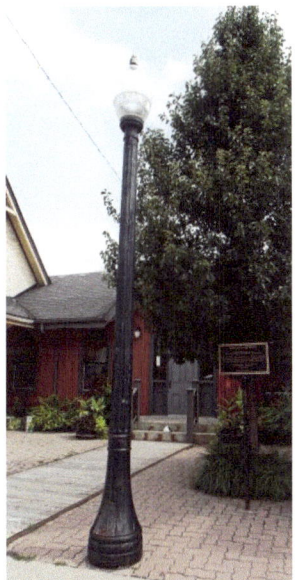

The lamp posts on this site were manufactured by The Beaver Foundry and Furnace Works, Tillsonburg in 1932.

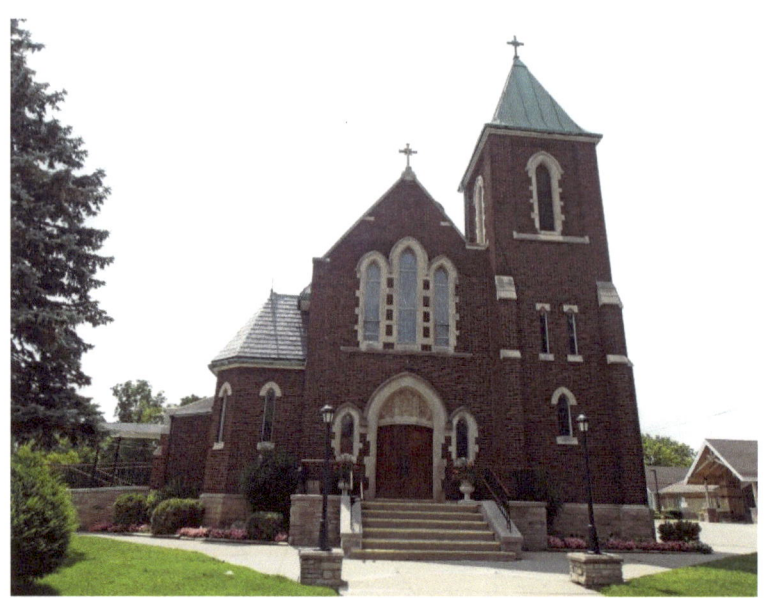

51 Venison Street West – St. Mary's Catholic Church

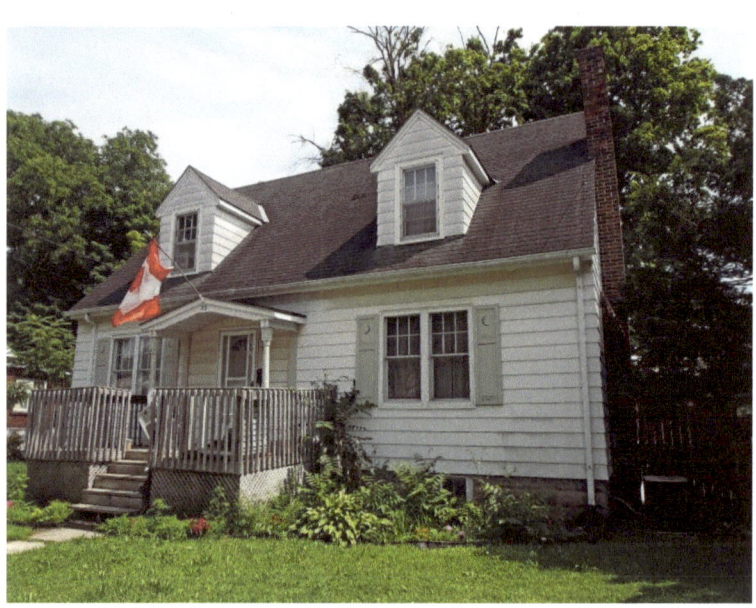

33 Venison Street West – dormers in attic

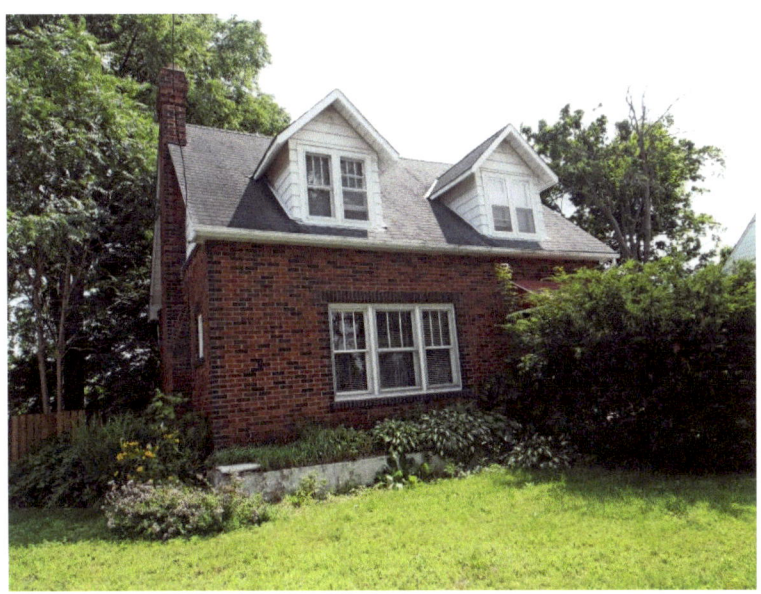

Venison Street West - dormers

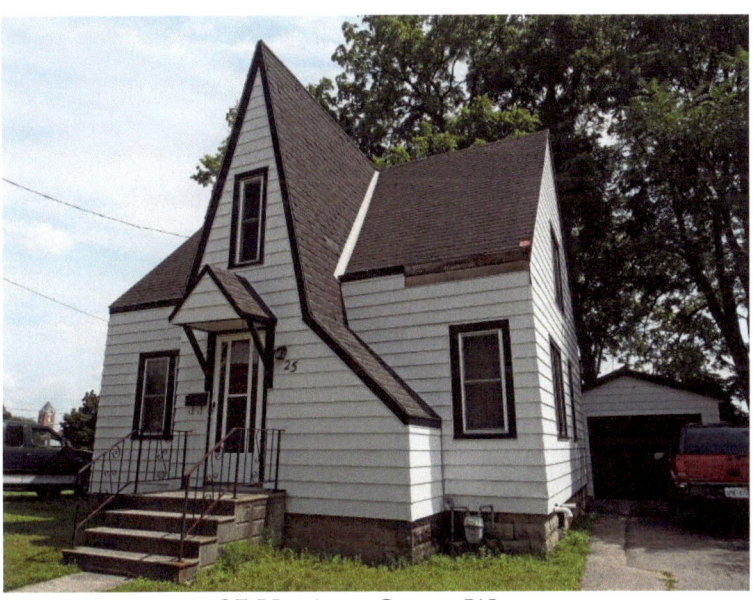

25 Venison Street West

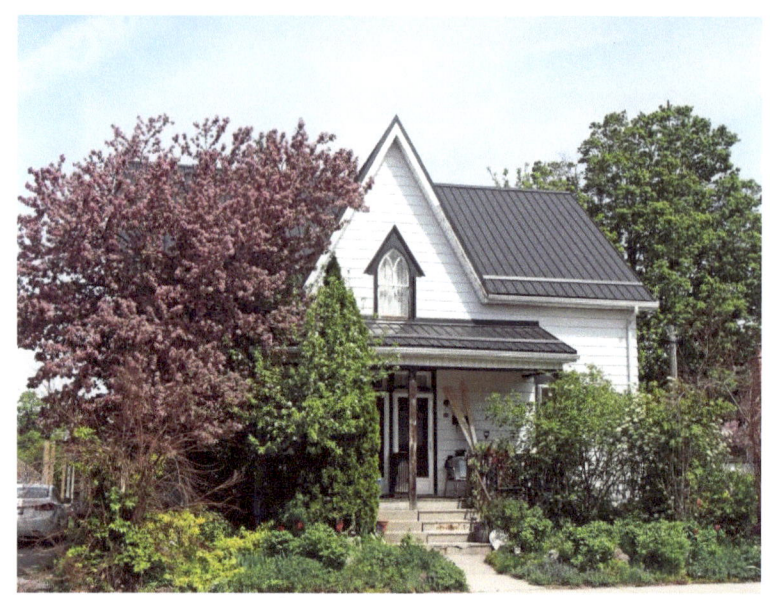

48 Washington Grand Avenue

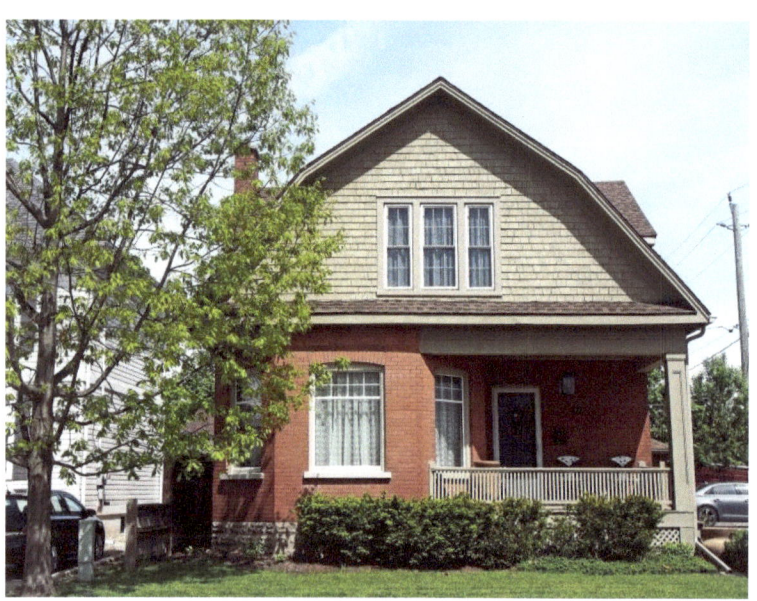

52 Washington Grand Avenue

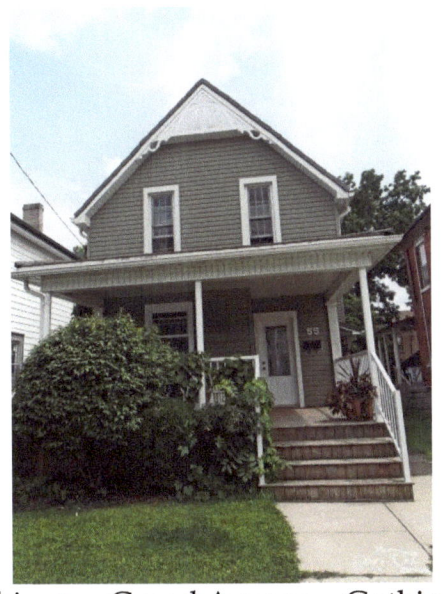

55 Washington Grand Avenue – Gothic Revival

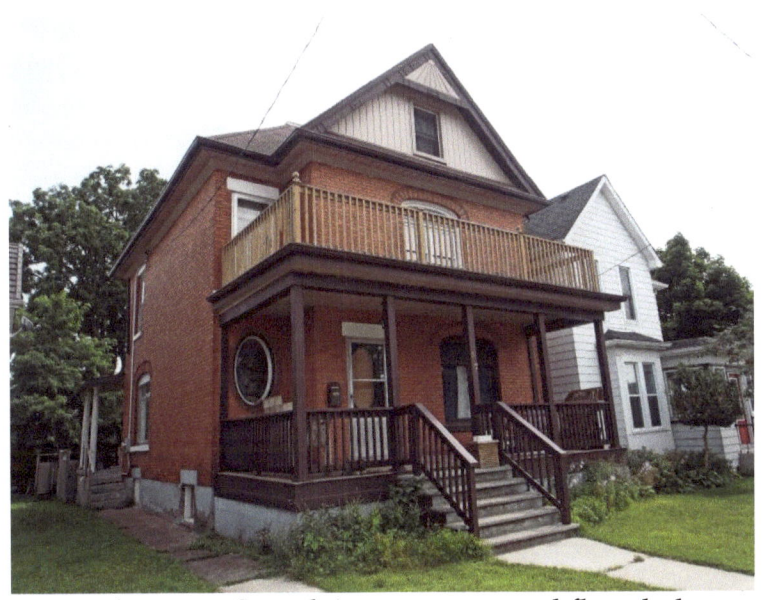

57 Washington Grand Avenue – second floor balcony

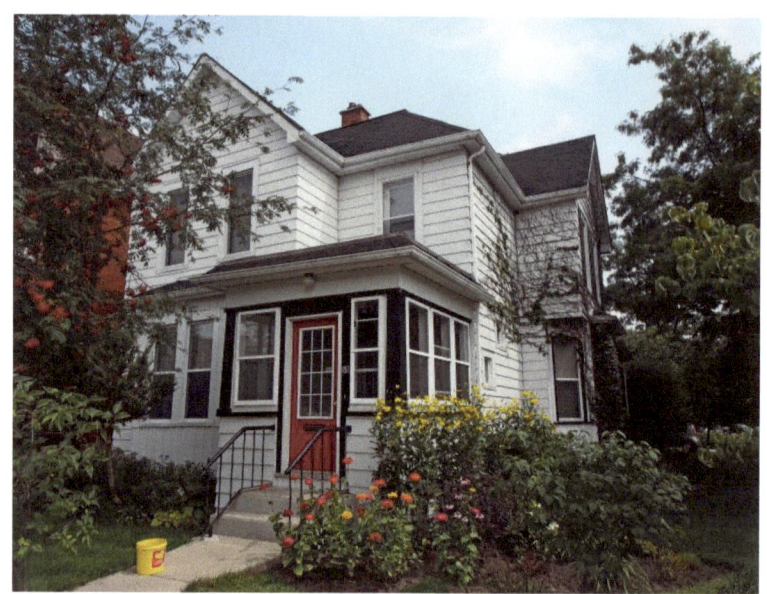

59 Washington Grand Avenue

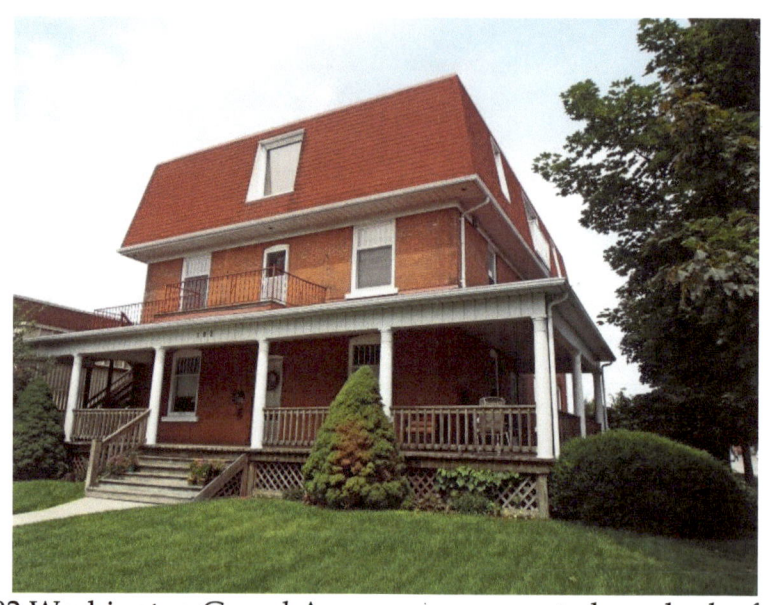

102 Washington Grand Avenue – appears to have had a full third floor added

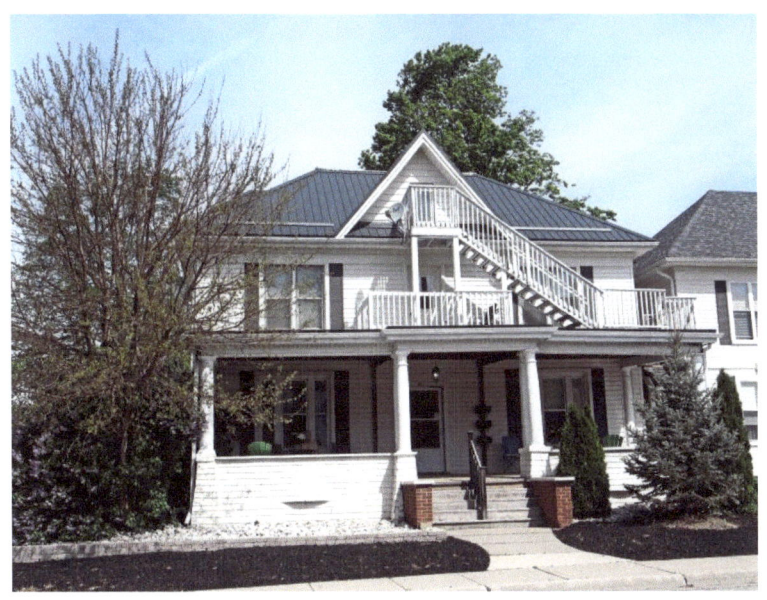

60 Washington Grand Avenue

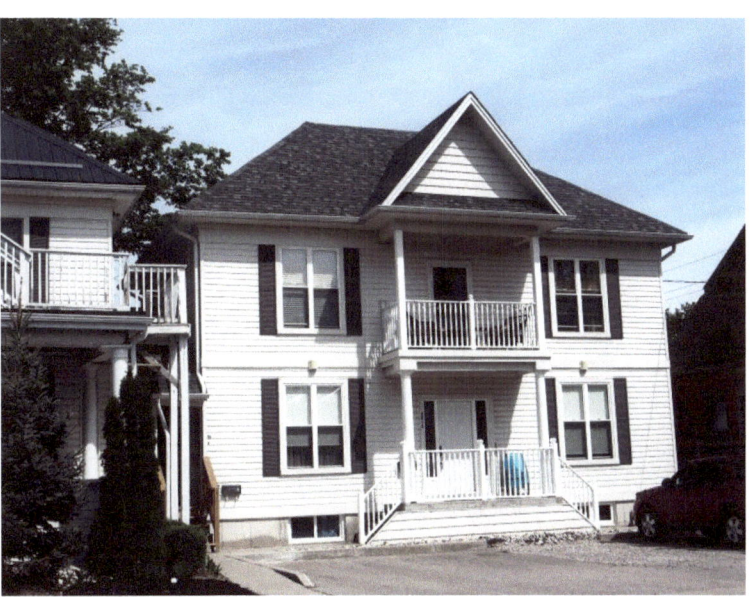

Apartments

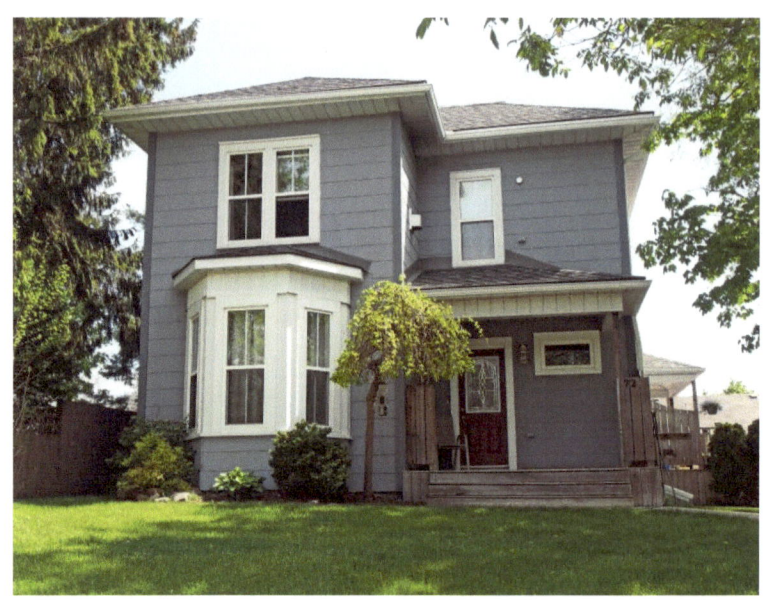

72 Rolph Street

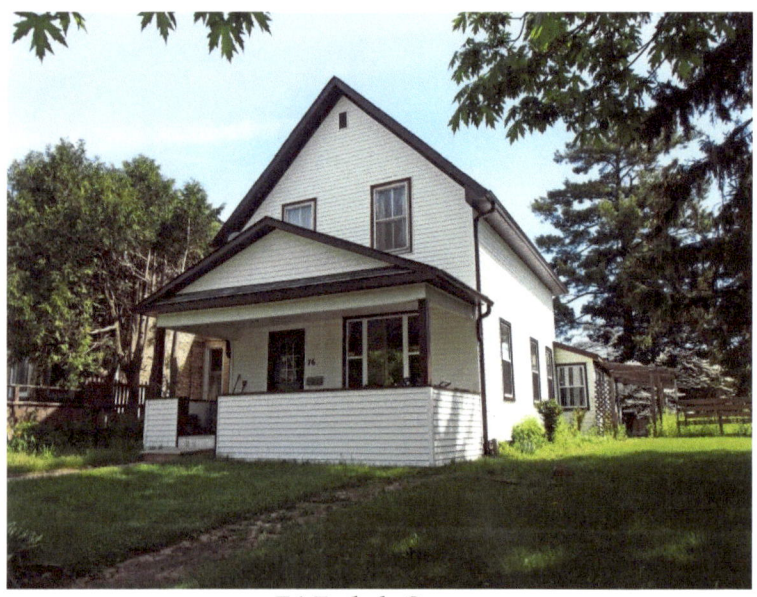

76 Rolph Street

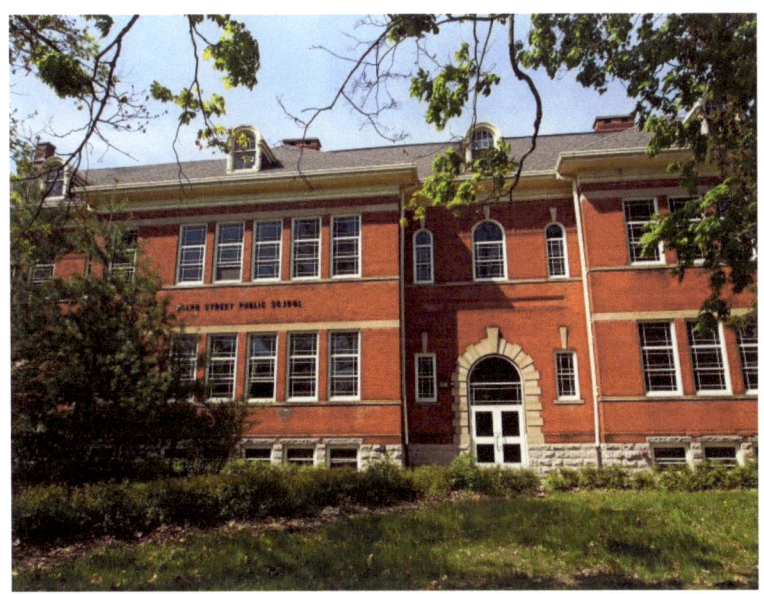

83 Rolph Street – Public School

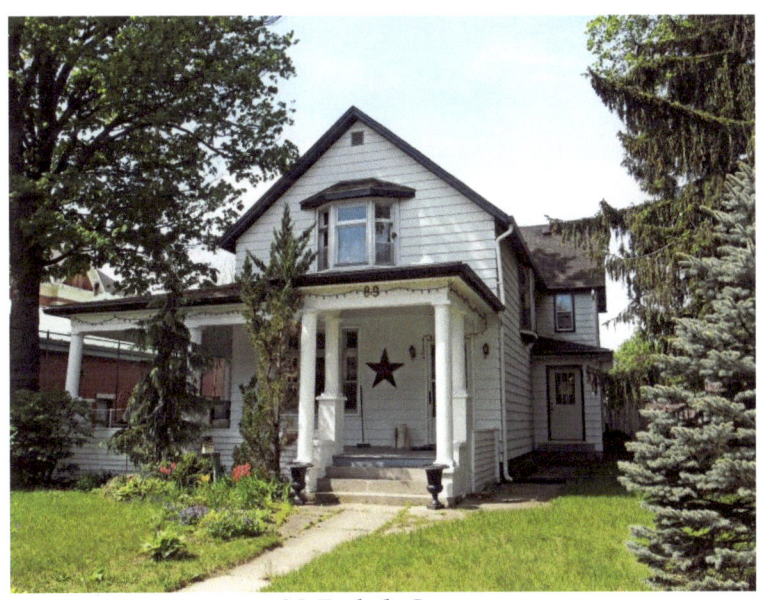

89 Rolph Street

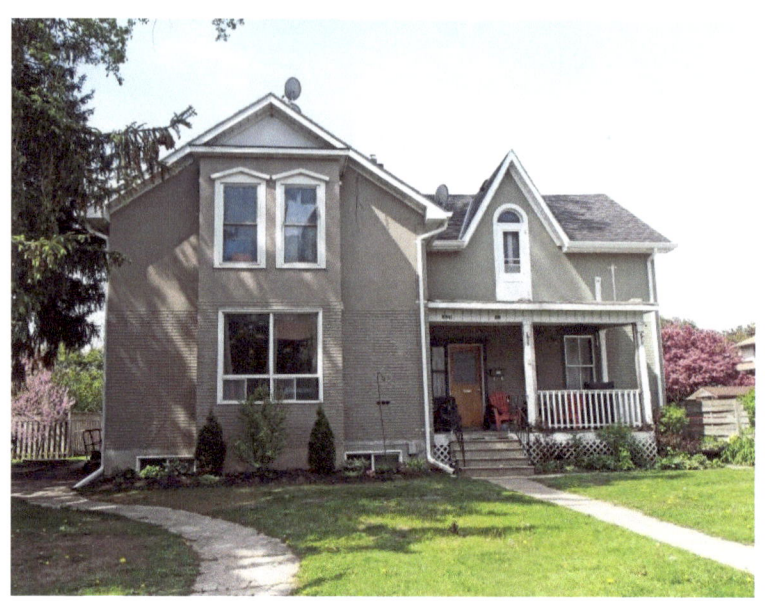

93-95 Rolph Street

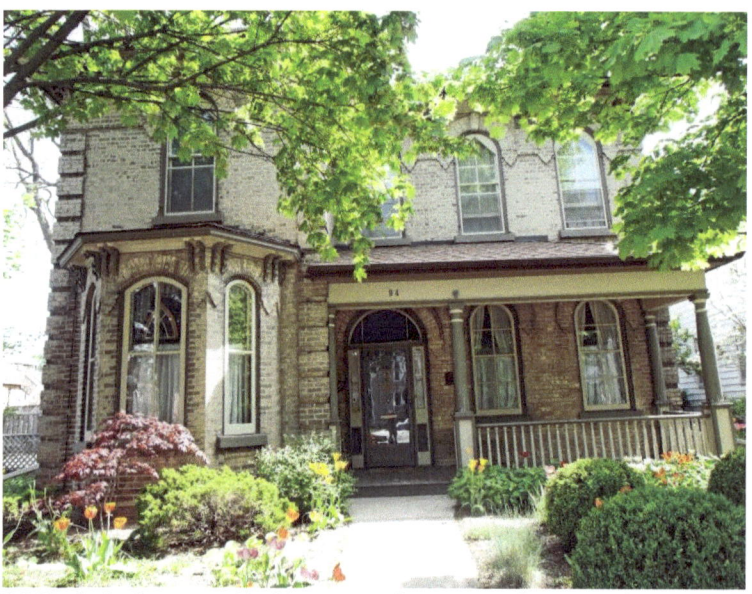

94 Rolph Street – Italianate – bay window with cornice brackets, corner quoins, voussoirs, keystones, sidelights and transom window

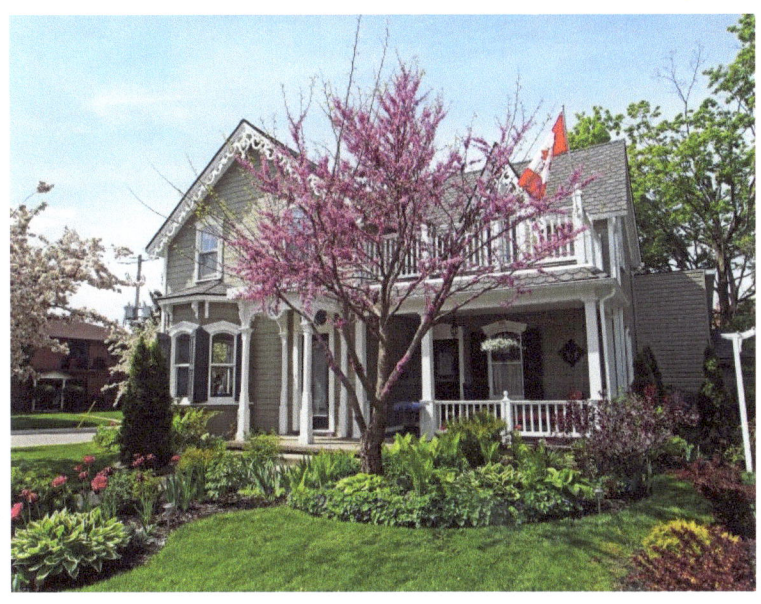

101 Rolph Street – Gothic Revival, verge board trim – heritage property

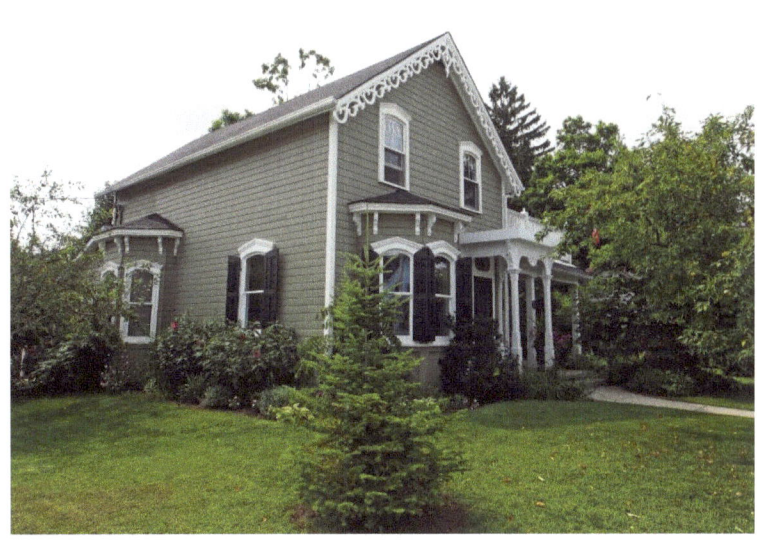

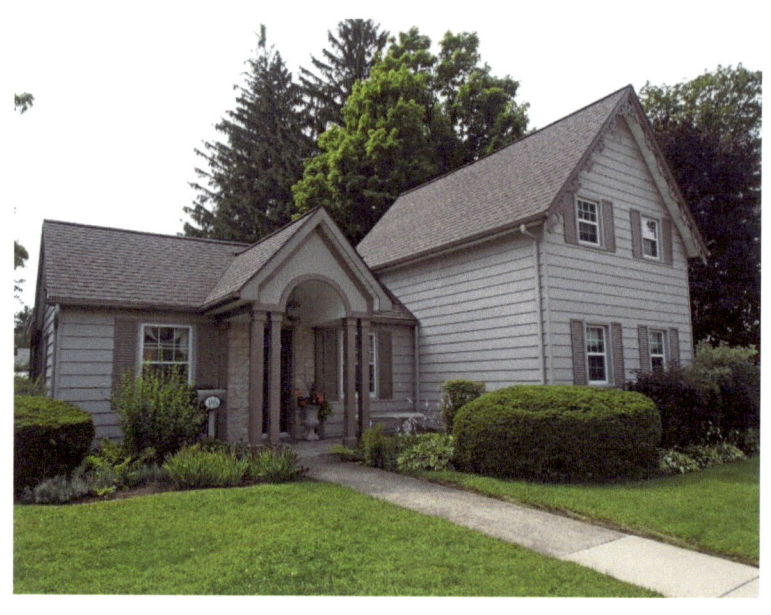

105 Rolph Street – Gothic Revival, verge board trim

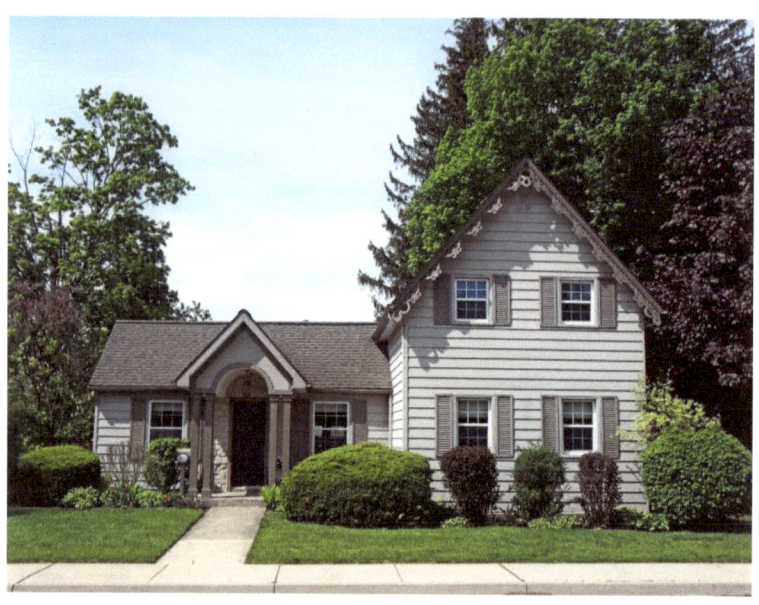

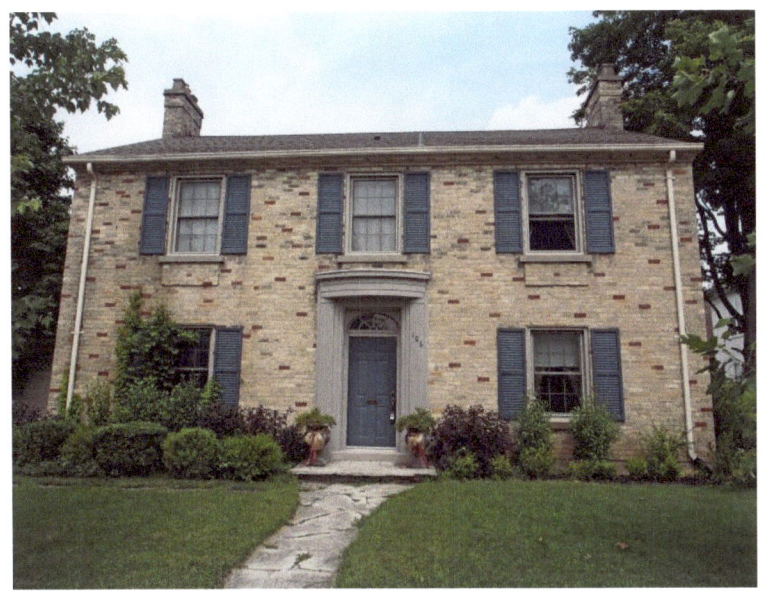

106 Rolph Street – Georgian style

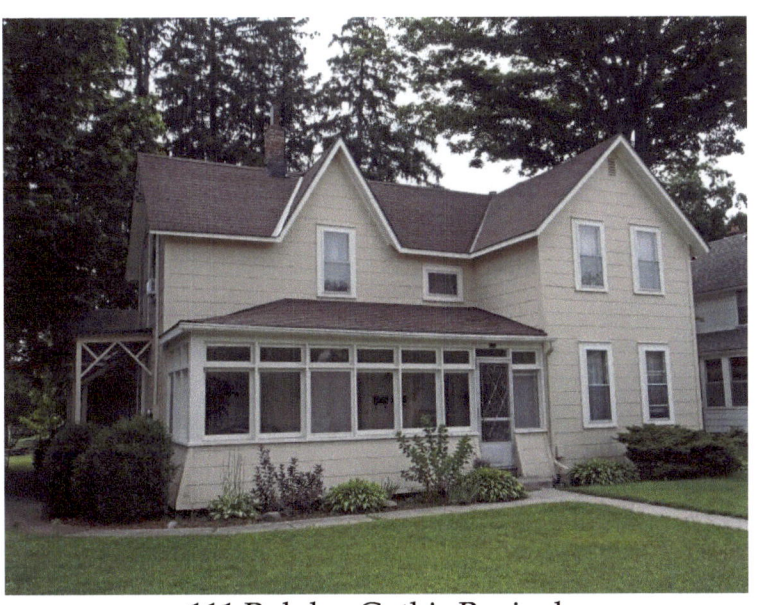

111 Rolph – Gothic Revival

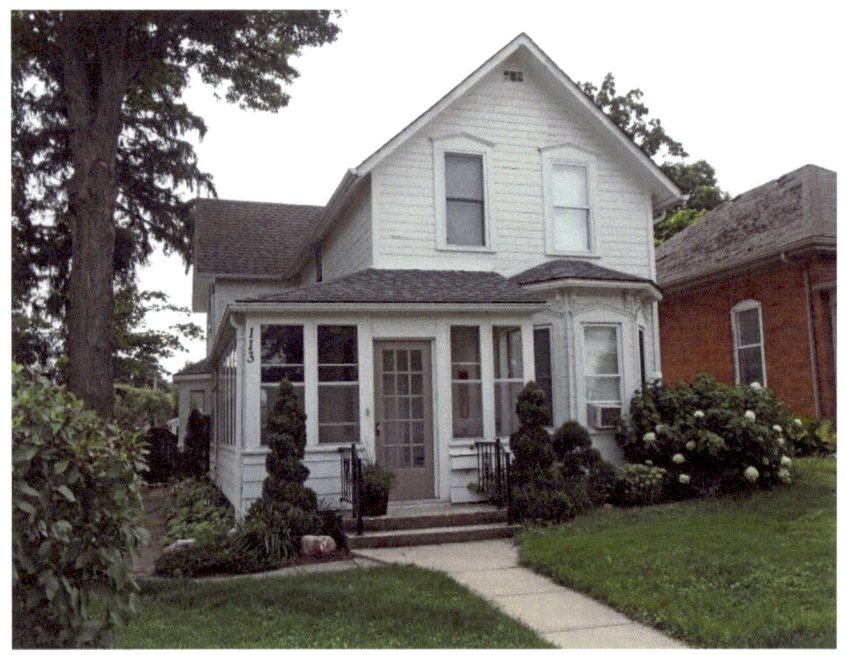

113 Rolph Street – Gothic Revival, bay window

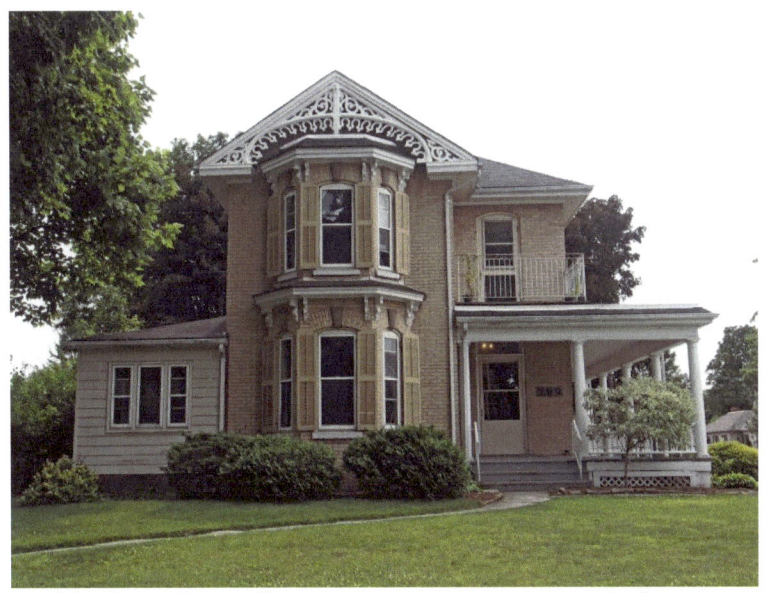

299 Broadway Street – two-storey bay windows,
cornice brackets, vergeboard trim

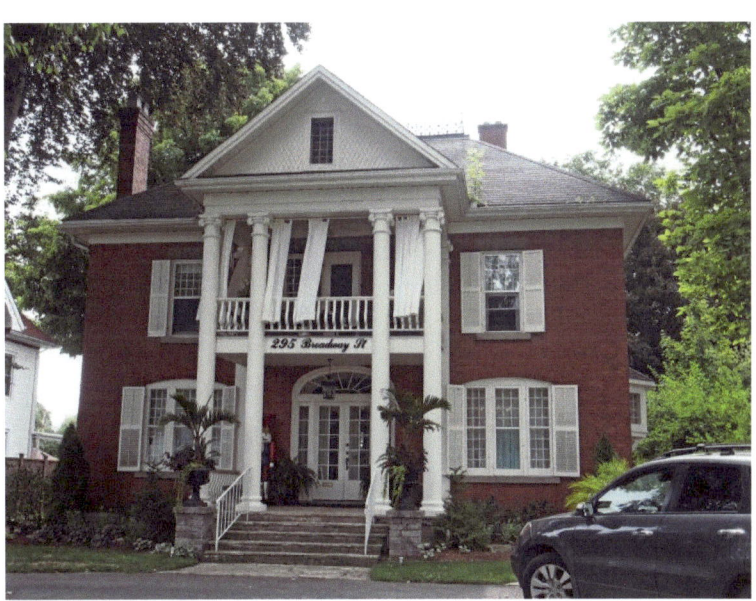

295 Broadway Street – two-storey high Ionic pillars

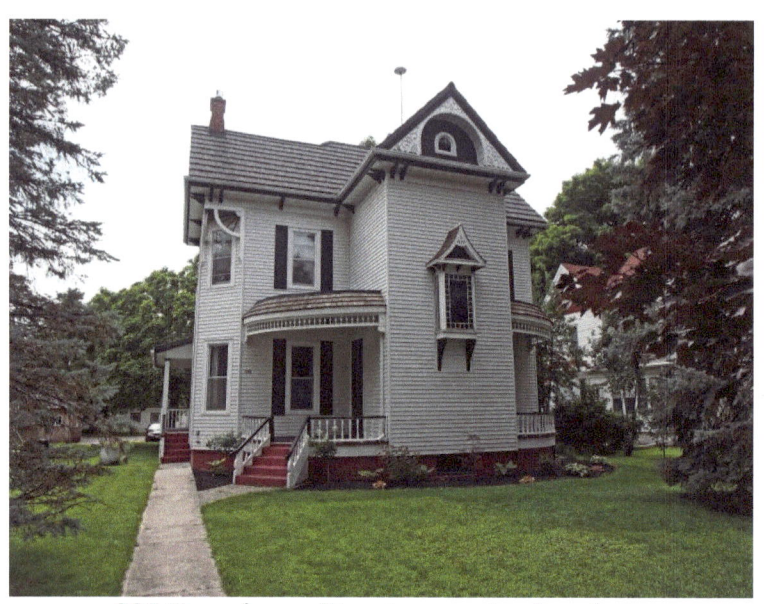

285 Broadway Street – cornice brackets

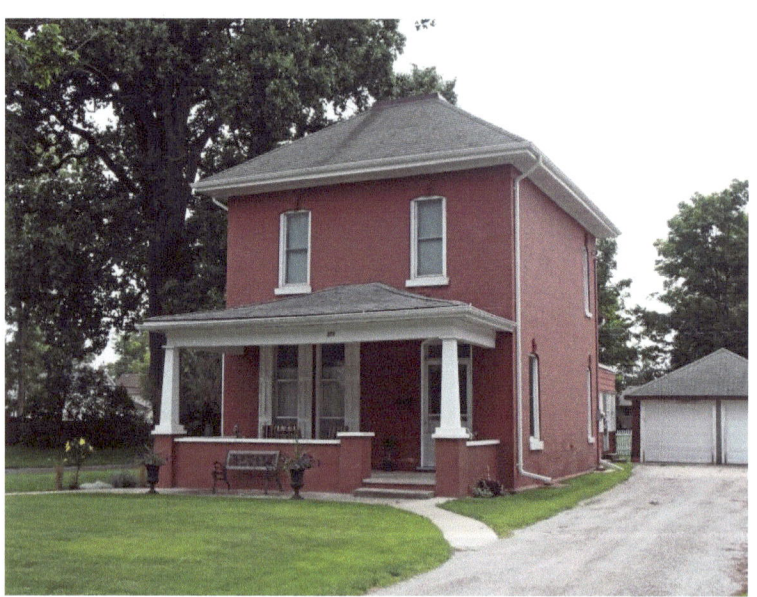

273 Broadway Street – Italianate, hipped roof

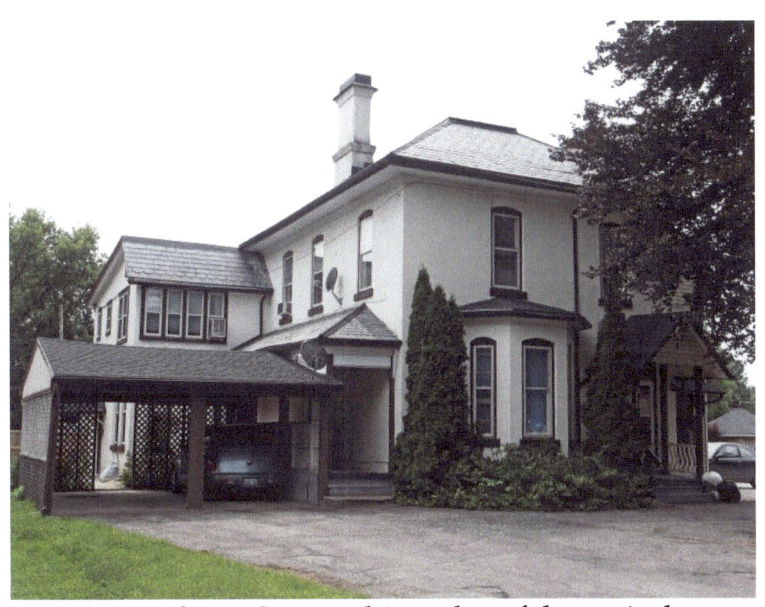

277 Broadway Street – hipped roof, bay window

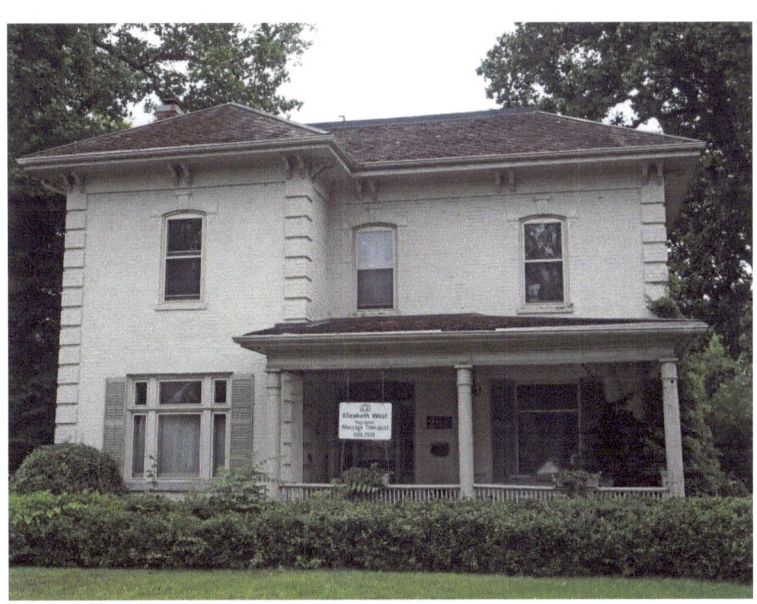

267 Broadway Street – Italianate, hipped roof, corner quoins,
Cornice brackets

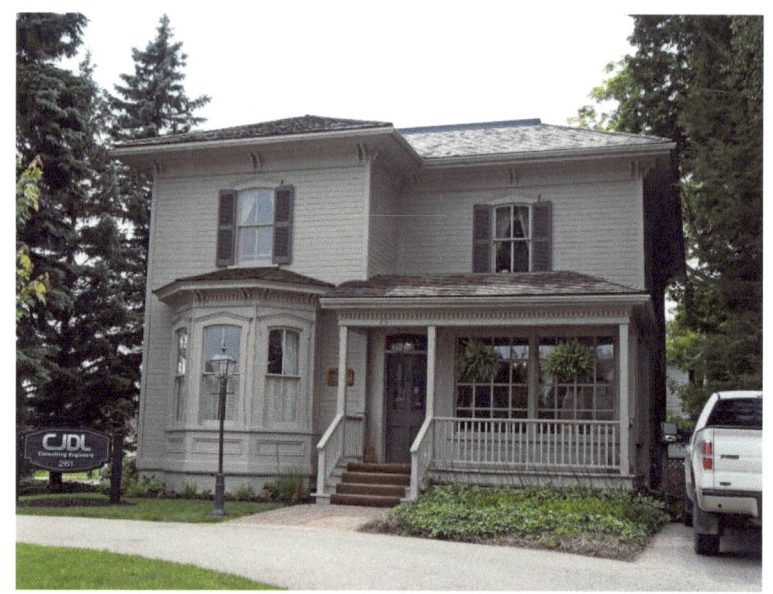

261 Broadway Street – Italianate, hipped roof, bay window

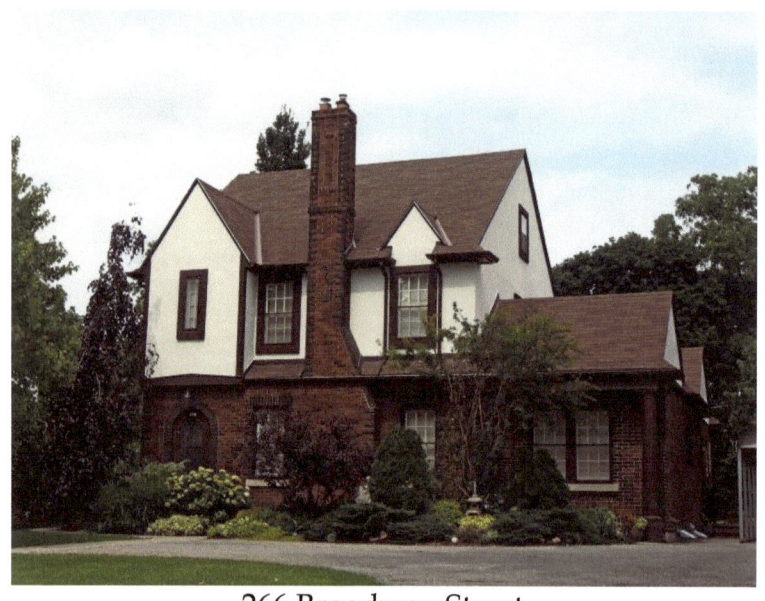

266 Broadway Street

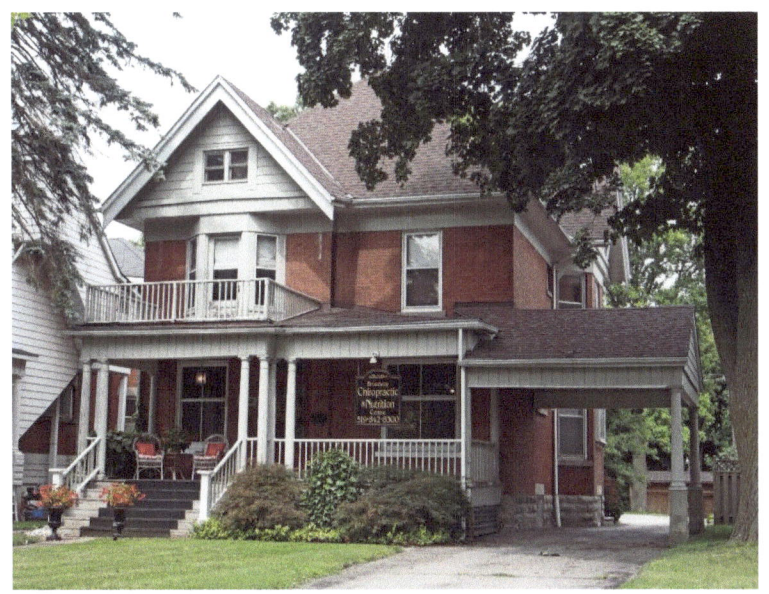

274 Broadway Street - Edwardian

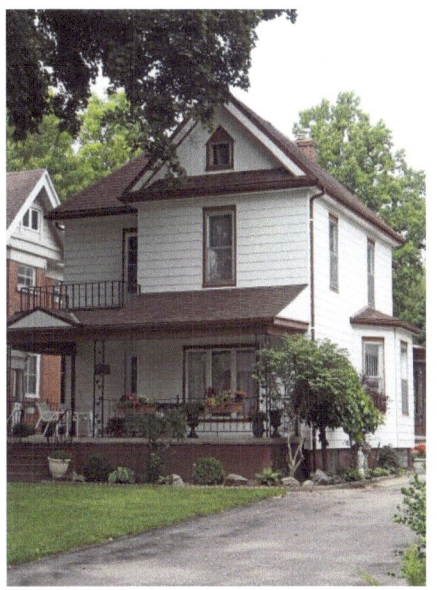

270 Broadway Street - Edwardian

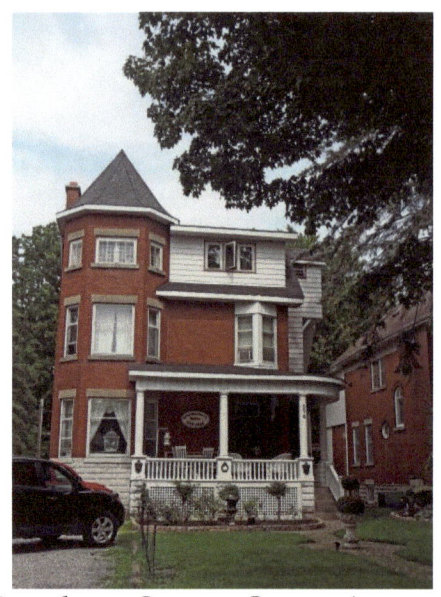

276 Broadway Street - Queen Anne, turret

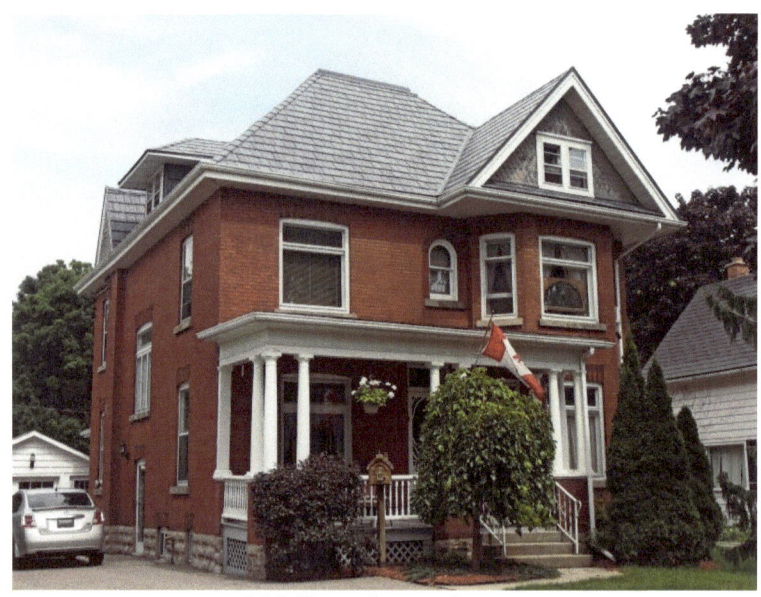

280 Broadway Street

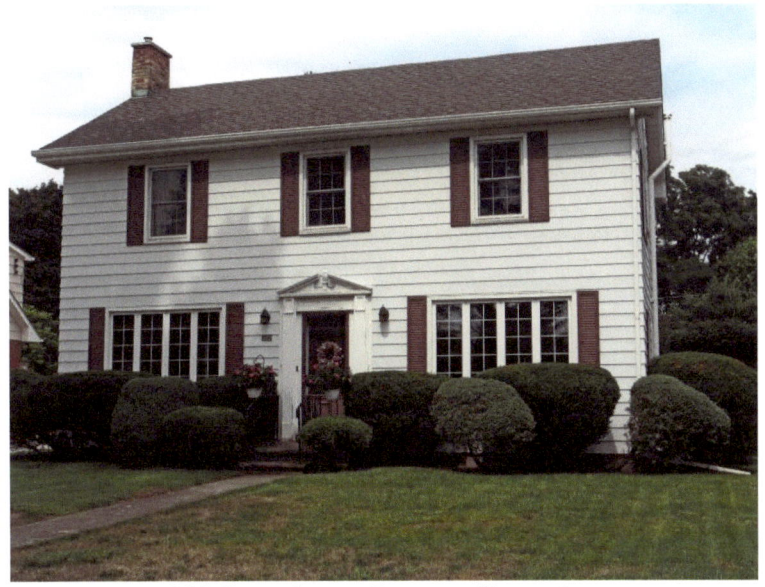

282 Broadway Street - Georgian

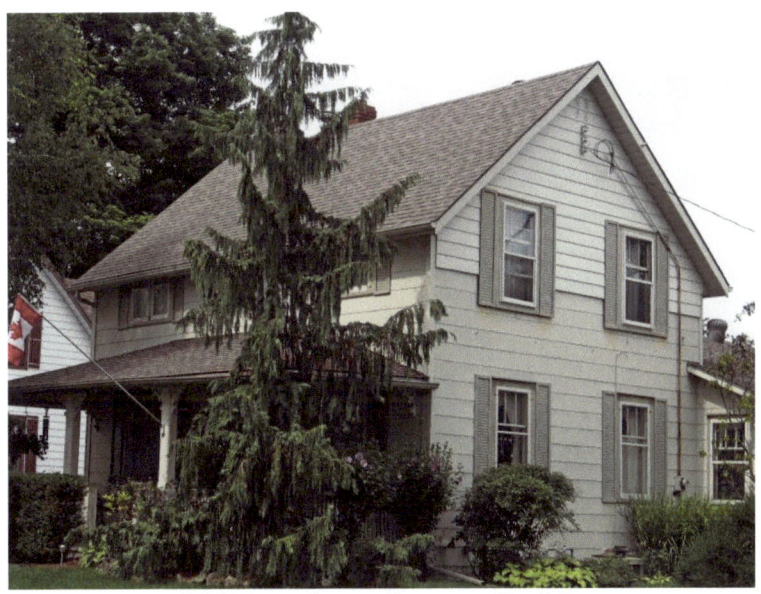

294 Broadway Street - Gothic

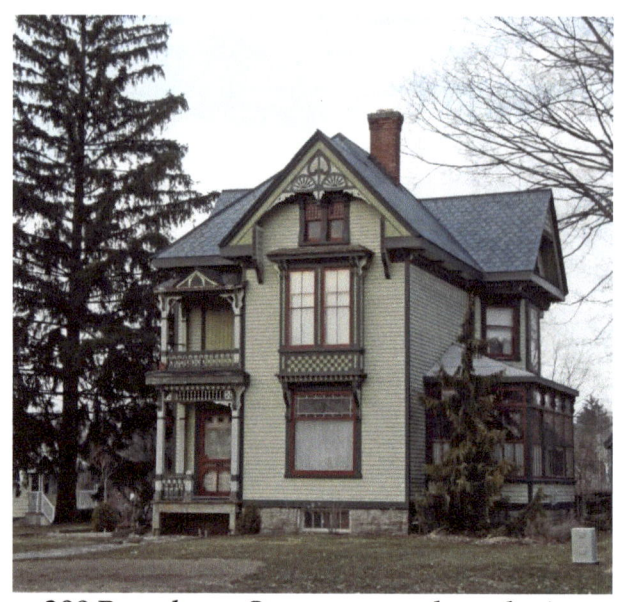

300 Broadway Street – vergeboard trim

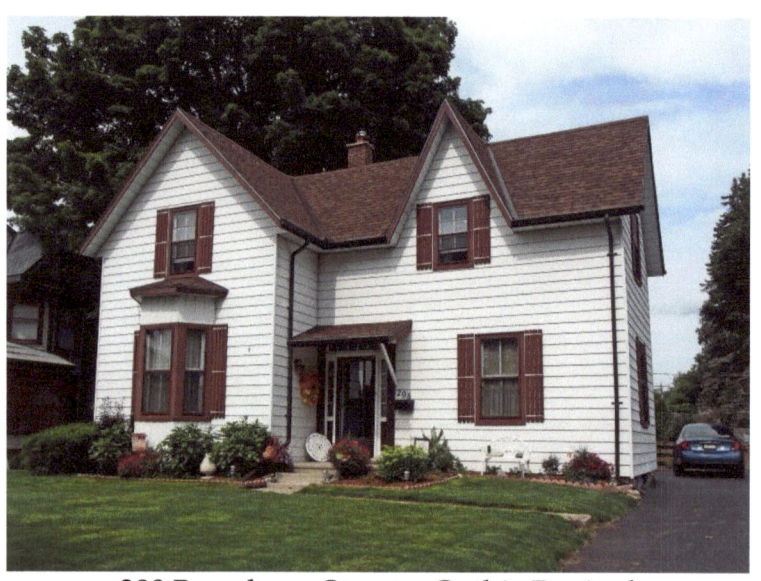

298 Broadway Street – Gothic Revival

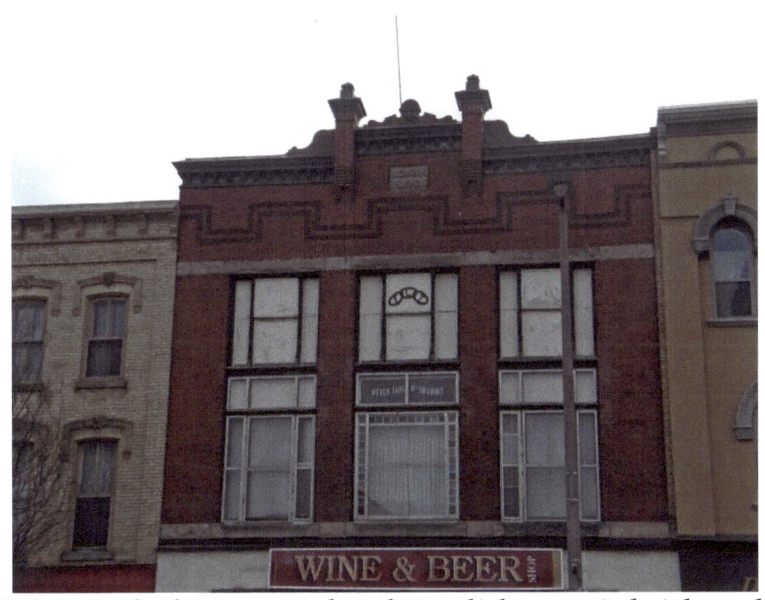

I.O.O.F. Block – cornice brackets, dichromatic brickwork

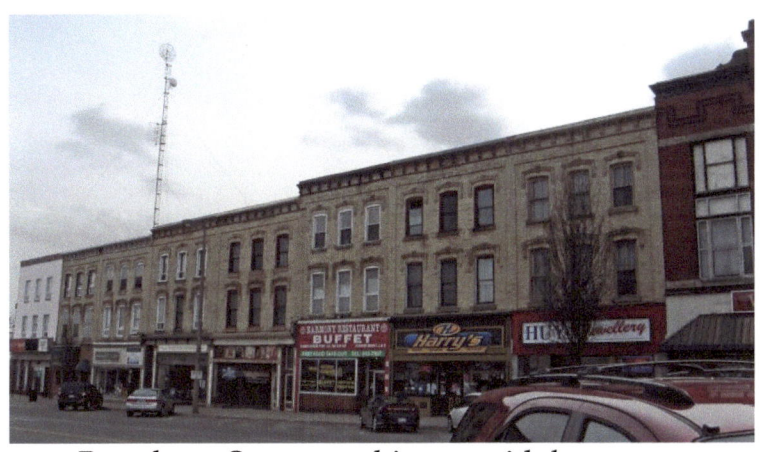

Broadway Street - architrave with keystones

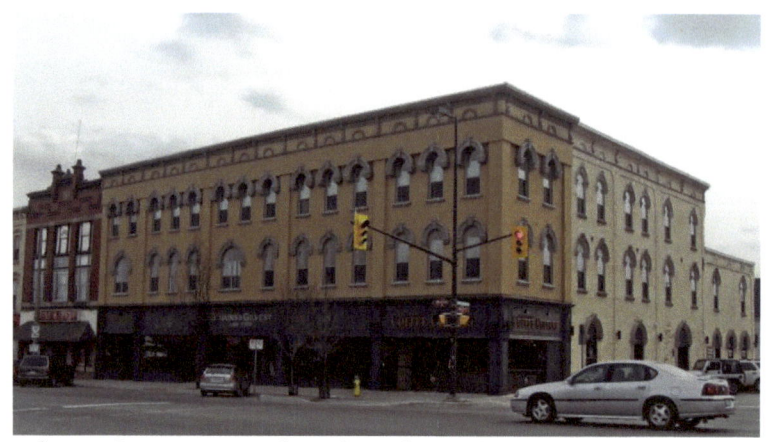

Broadway Street - window hoods with keystones on top floor

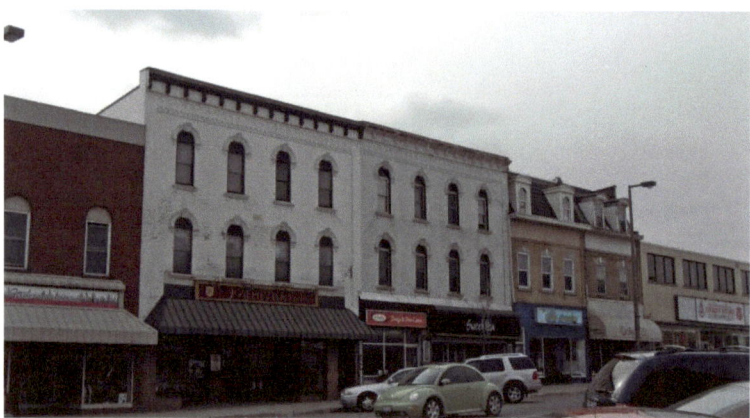

Broadway Street - dentil moulding – dormers to right

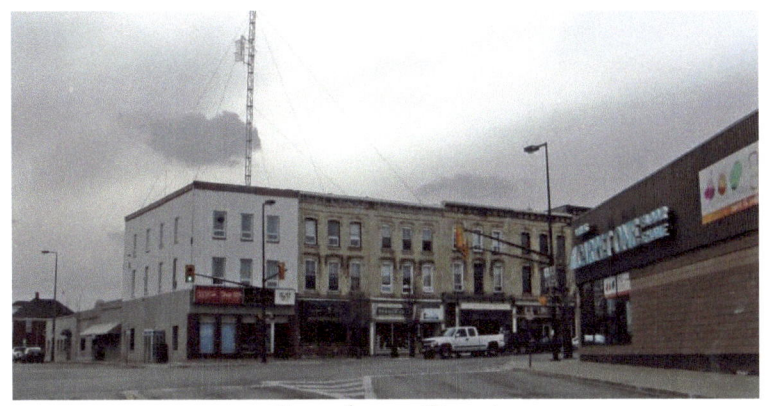

Broadway Street

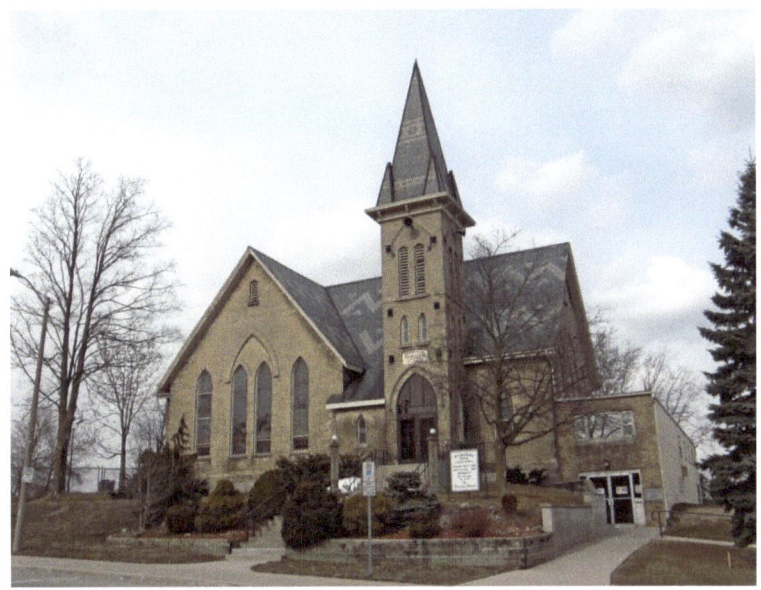

60 Harvey Street – Avondale United Zion Church - dichromatic tile work, lancet windows

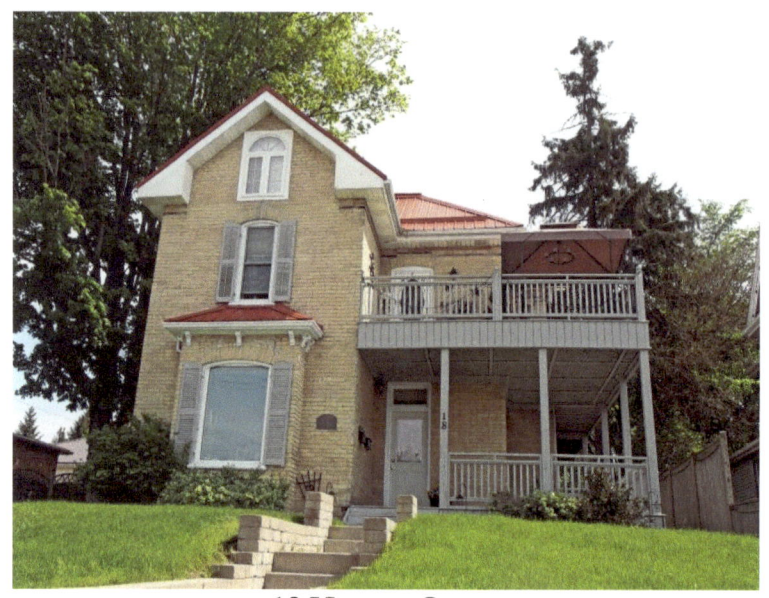

18 Harvey Street

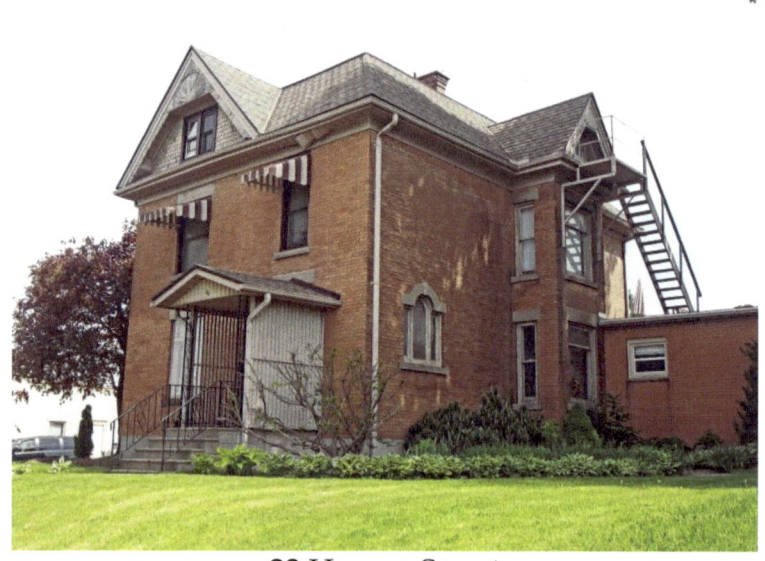

22 Harvey Street

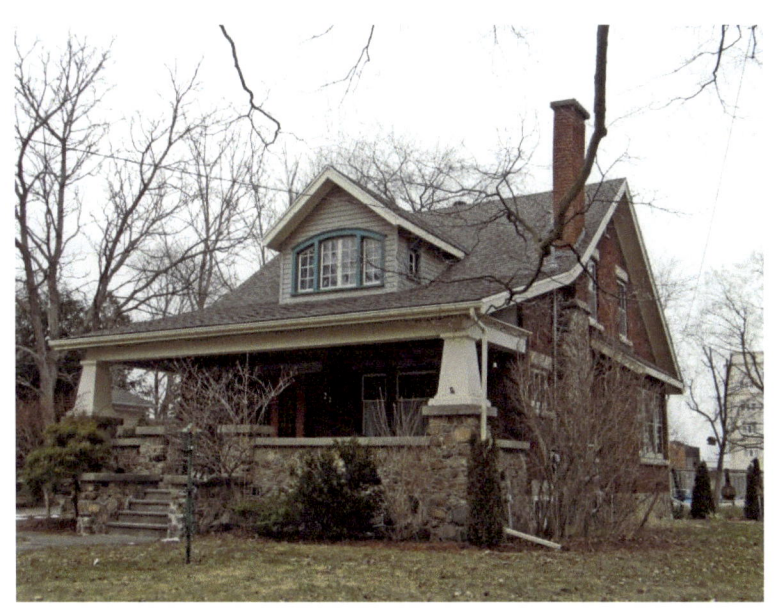

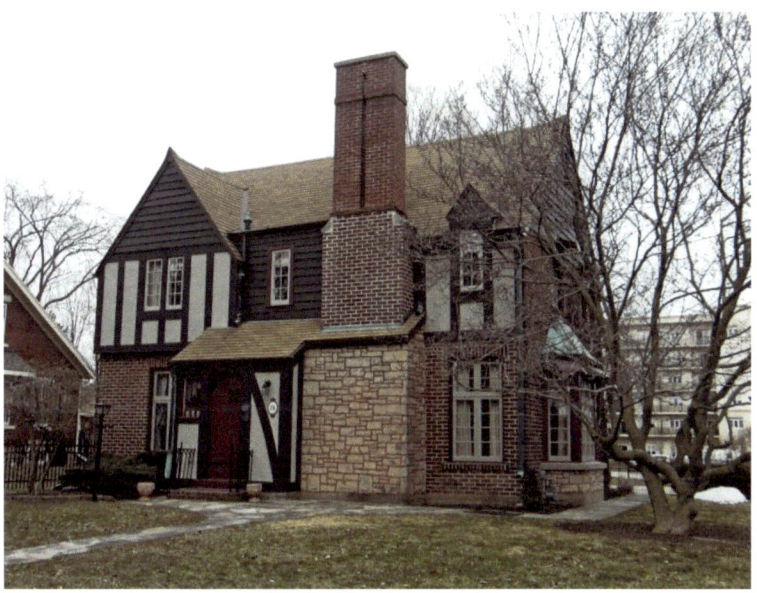

#16 - Tudor style

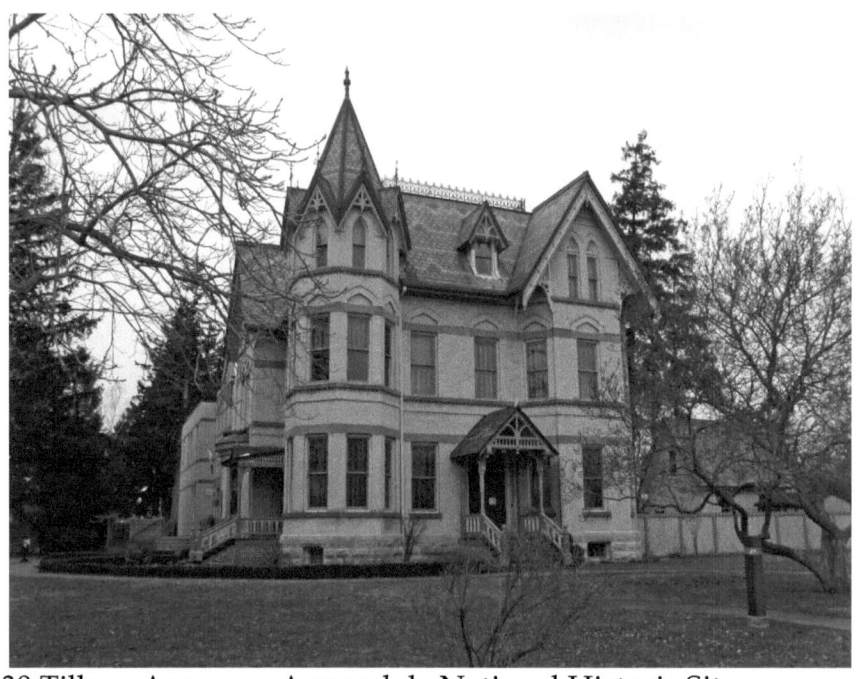

30 Tillson Avenue – Annandale National Historic Site
Constructed in seven years in the 1880s, this was the farm
house for E.D. Tillson's 600-acre Model Farm. The interior of
the house exemplifies the Victorian style of design known as
the "Aesthetic Art Movement" which was popularized by
Oscar Wilde, and encouraged the use of color and decorative
detailing. There are hand-painted ceilings, elaborate inlaid
floors, ornate mantles, and stained glass throughout.

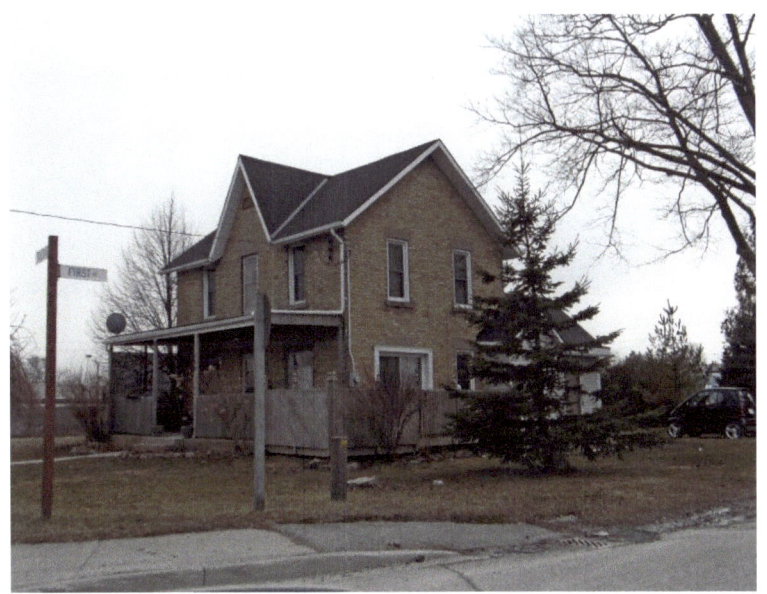

First Street

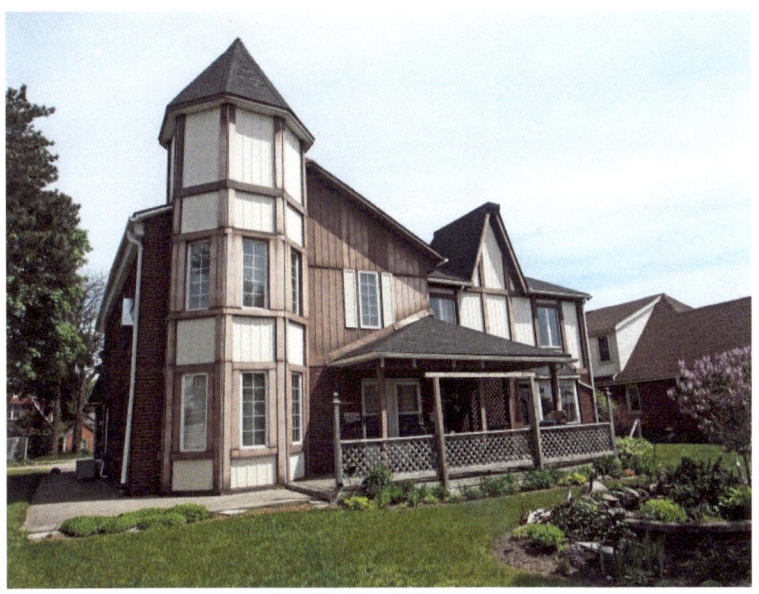

48 Oxford Street

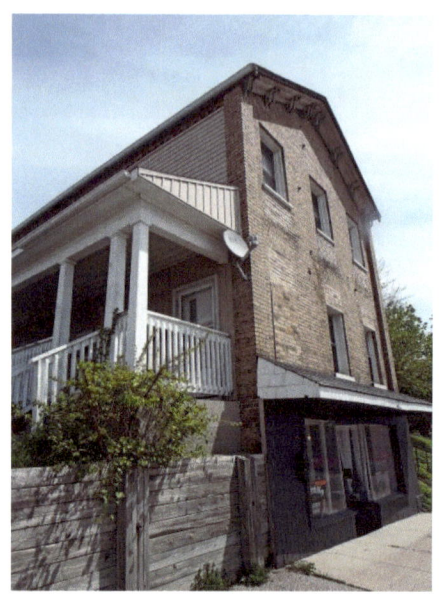

42 Oxford Street

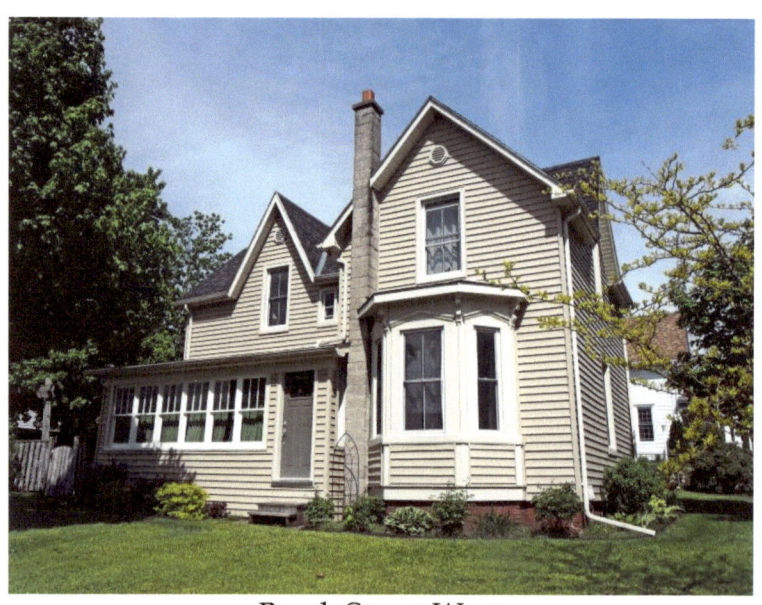

Brock Street West

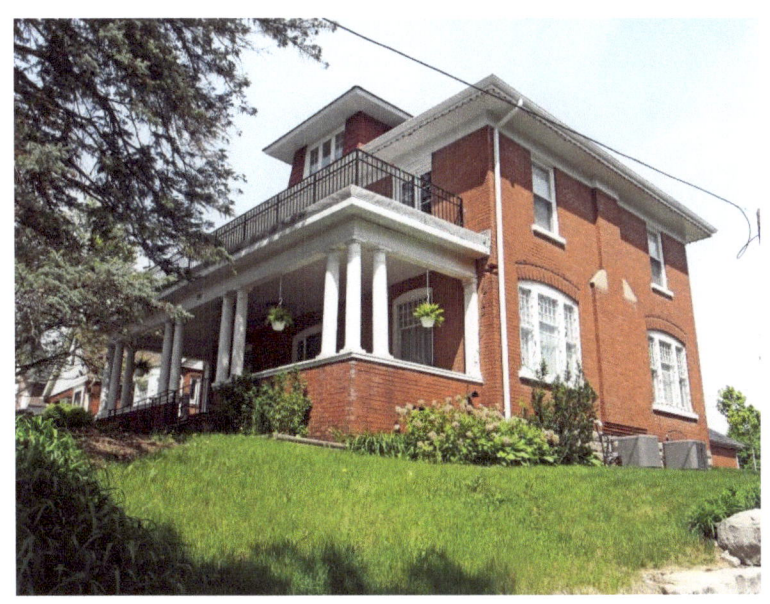

56 Oxford Street

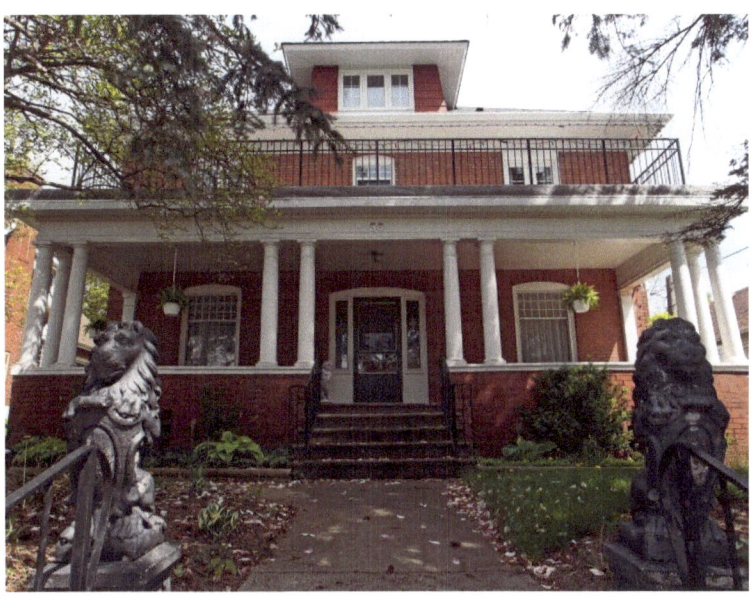

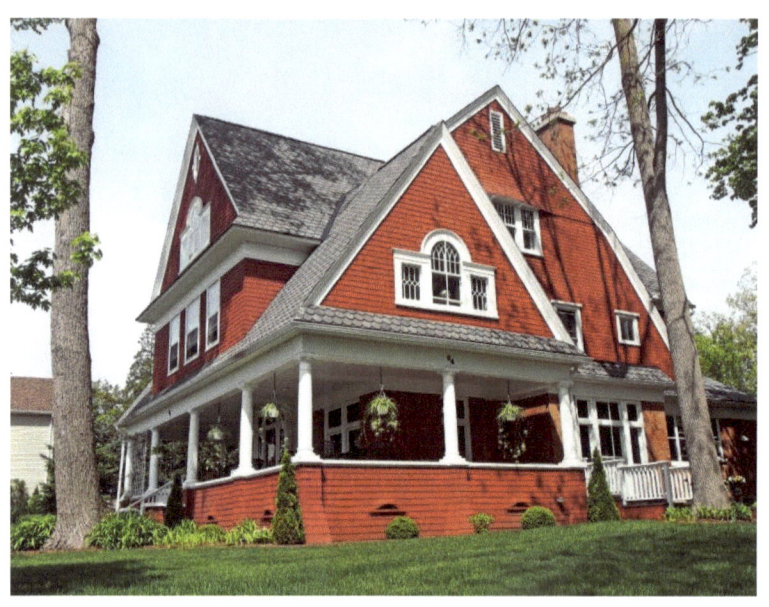

64 Oxford Street – Seven Gables Bed & Breakfast

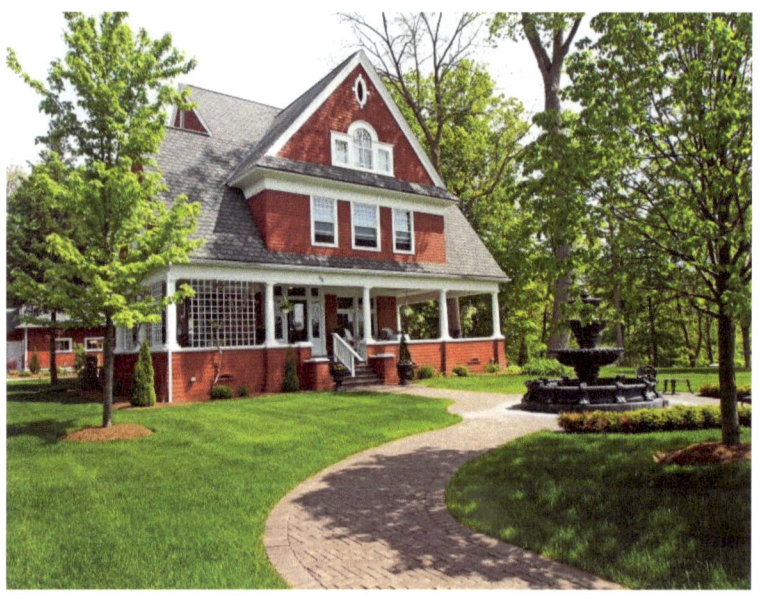

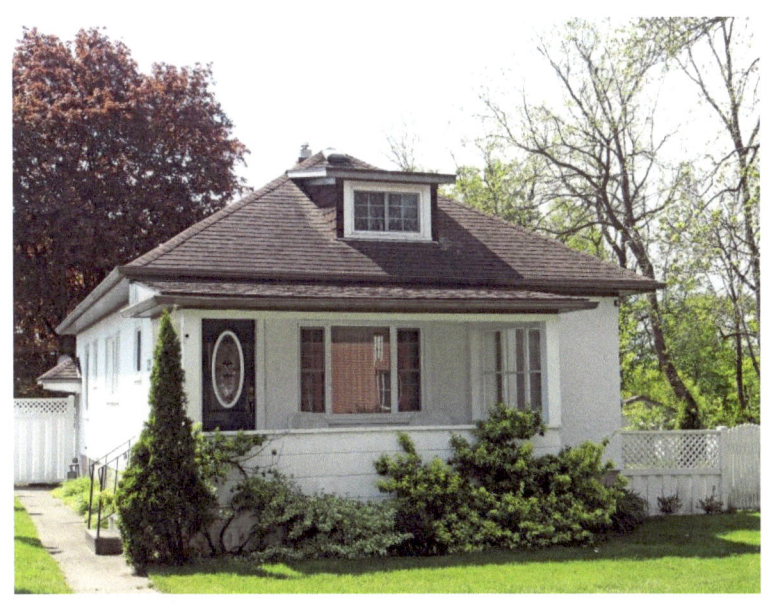

Brock Street West

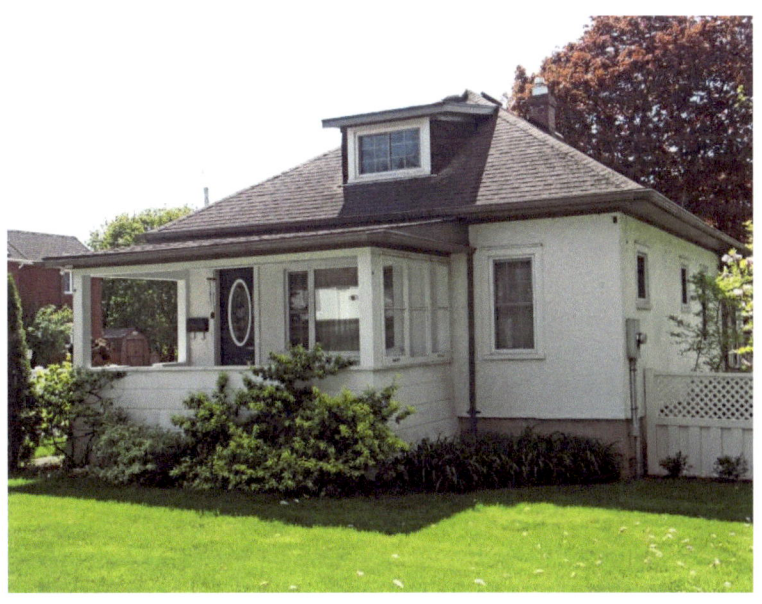

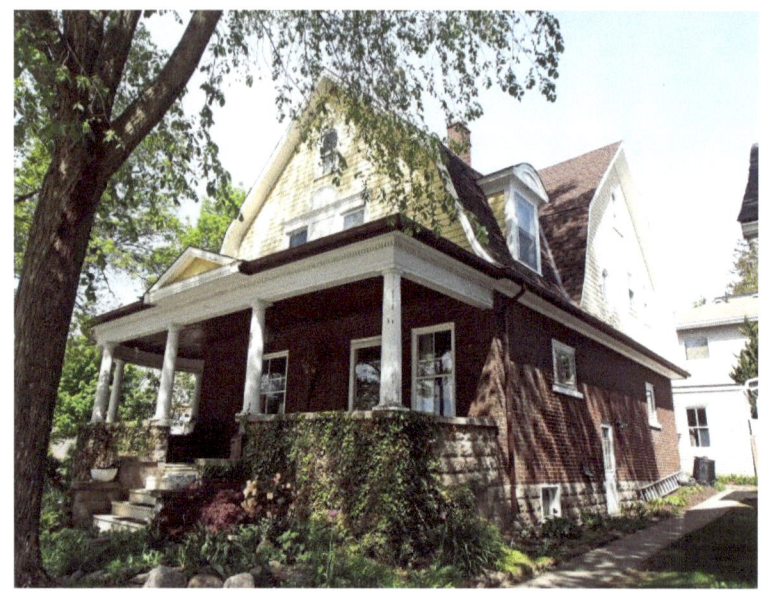

60 Brock Street West – Neo-Colonial – gambrel roofs

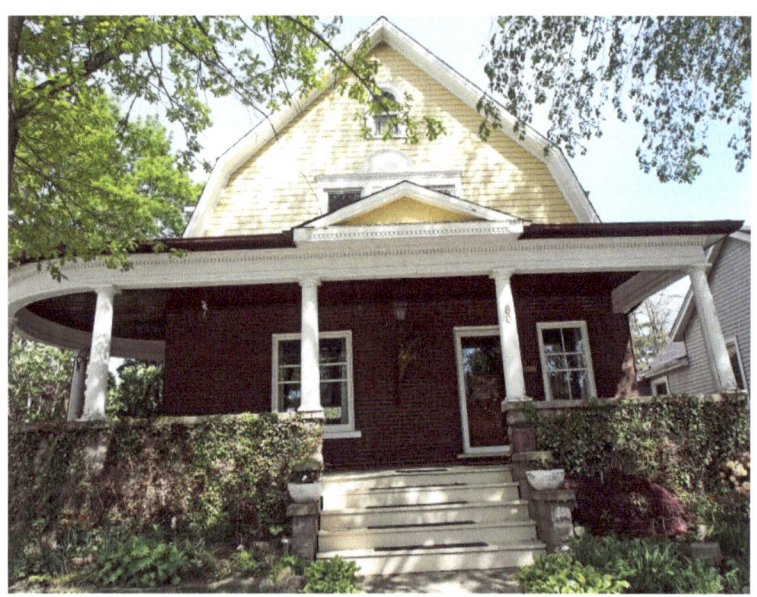

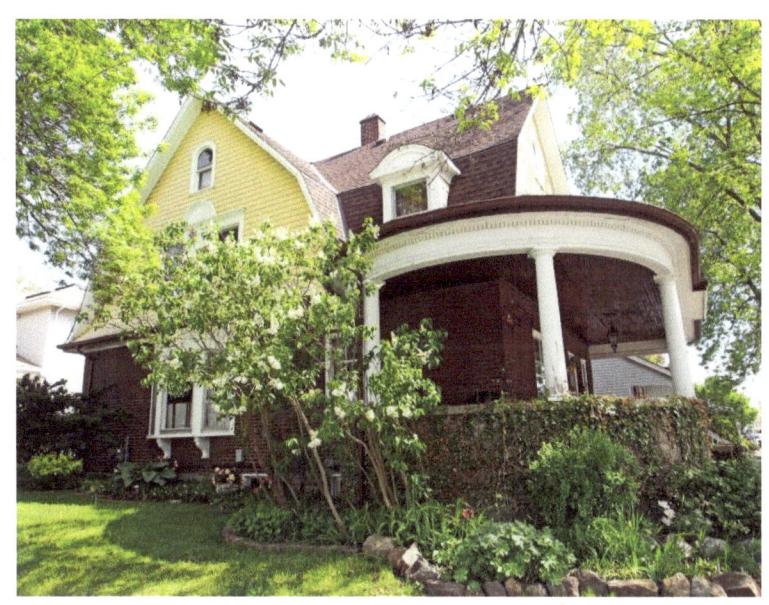

60 Brock Street West – Neo-Colonial – gambrel roofs

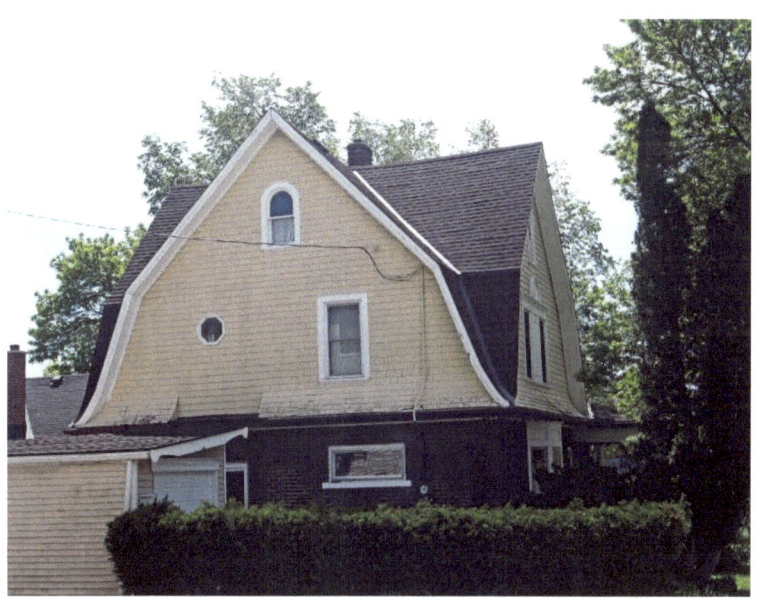

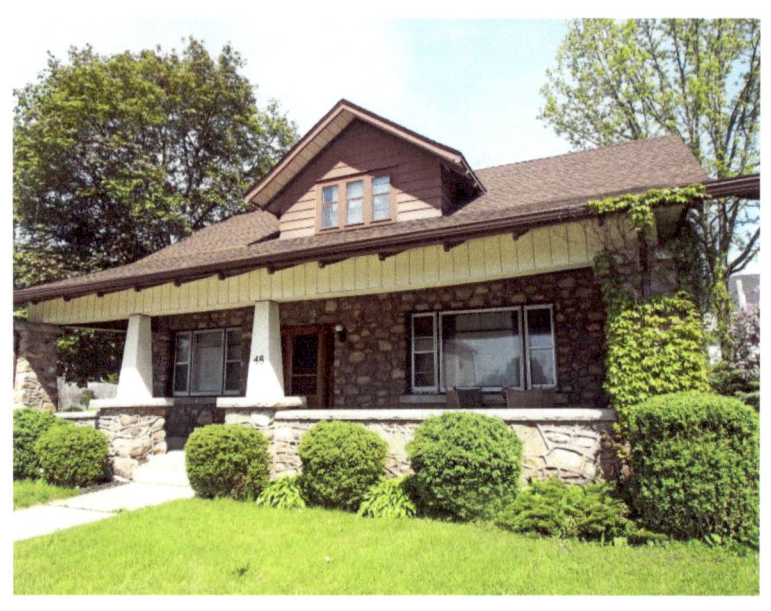

48 Brock Street West

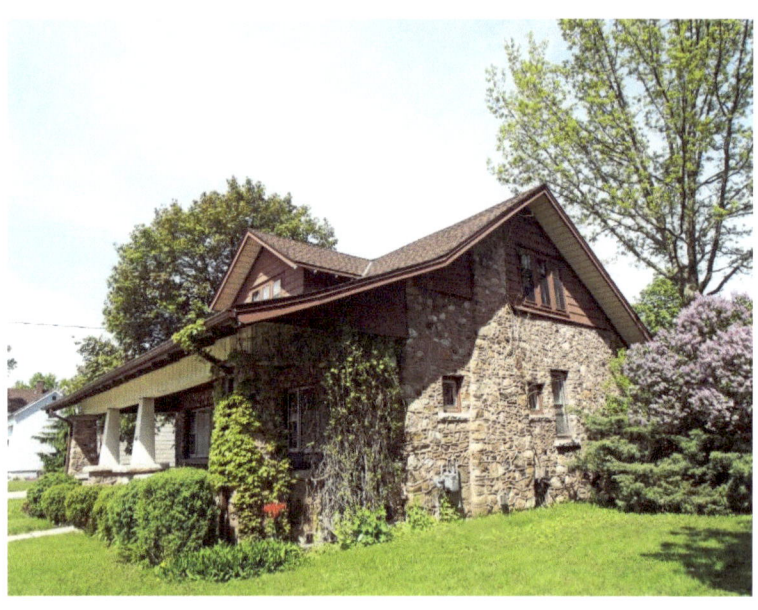

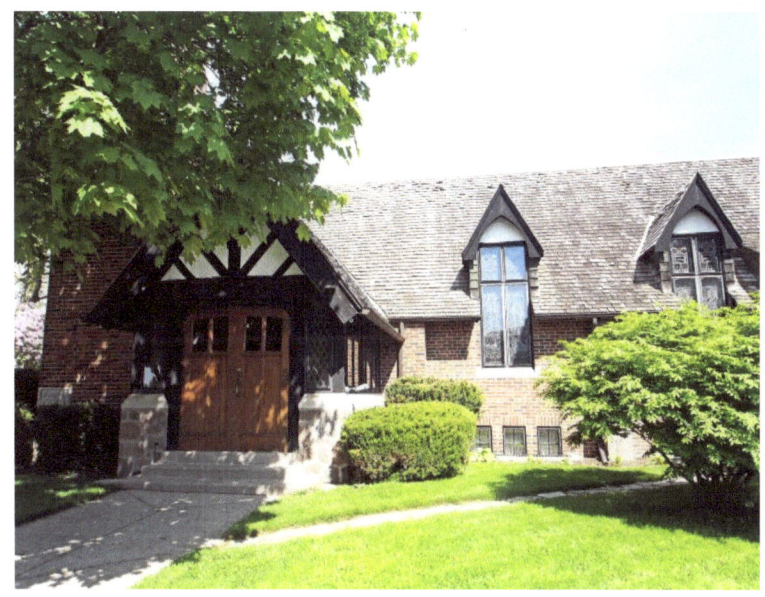

46 Brock Street West – St. Andrew's Presbyterian Church

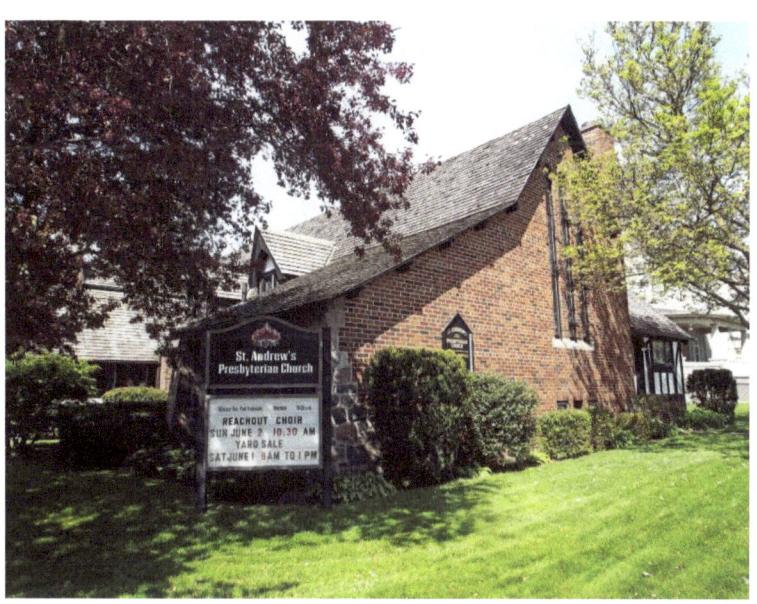

Architectural Terms

Brackets: a decorative or weight-bearing structural element which forms a right angle with one side against a wall and the other under a projecting surface such as an eave or roof. Example: 299 Broadway Street, Page 31	
Cornice: originally the wooden overhang of the roof. With the use of stone, brick, iron and steel, the cornice is any projecting shelf at the top of a ceiling or roof. They can be very decorative. Example: 105 Rolph Street, Page 28	
Dentil Moulding: an even series of rectangles used as ornamental decoration in cornices. Example: Broadway Street, Page 40	
Dichromatic brickwork: the use of two colours of brick, tile or slate to decorate a façade. Example: IOOF Block, Page 39	
Dormer: (French for "sleep") a gable end window that pierces through the plane of a sloping roof surface to create usable space in the top floor or attic of a building by adding headroom. Example: 83 Bidwell Street, Page 14	
Gable: the triangular portion of a wall between the edges of a sloping roof. Example: 107 Bidwell Street, Page 10	
Hipped Roof: a roof where all sides slope downwards to the walls with no gables. Example: 97 Bidwell Street, Page 13	

Keystones and Voussoirs: a voussoir is a wedge-shaped element used in building an arch. A keystone is the central stone that locks all the stones into position, allowing the arch to bear weight. A keystone is often enlarged and embellished. Example: Broadway, Page 39	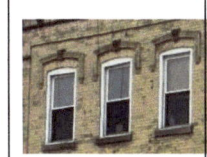
Lancet Window: a tall, narrow window with a pointed arch at its top. Example: 46 Ridout Street West, Page 5	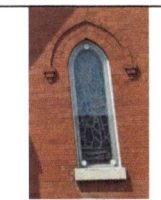
Quoin: masonry blocks at the corner of a wall, often a decorative feature, usually larger or of a different colour than the rest of the wall. Example: 267 Broadway Street, Page 33	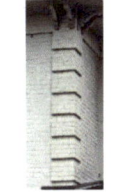
Turret: a small tower that projects from the wall of a building. Example: 276 Broadway Street, Page 36	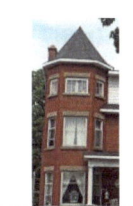
Vergeboard and Finial: also called bargeboards – hang from the projecting end of a roof and are often elaborately carved and ornamented. **Finial:** ornament added to the top of a gable, pinnacle, canopy or spire – a Gothic element. Example: 140 Bidwell Street, Page 12	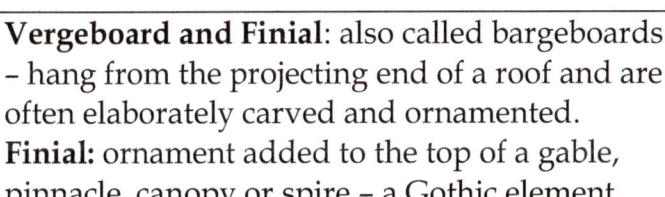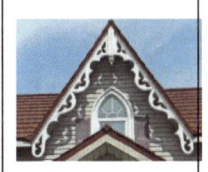
Window Hood: A **hood** is the piece found above window openings, usually of an ornate design, and covers the top third of the opening. Hoods are commonly placed above arched or curved openings on both windows and doors. Example: Broadway Street, Page 40	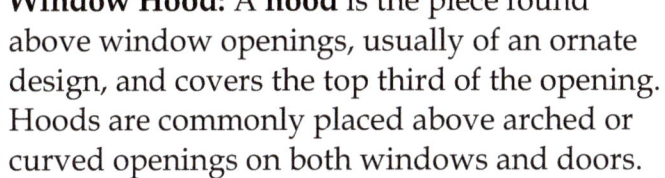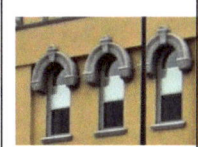

Edwardian, 1900-1930 – This style bridges the ornate and elaborate styles of the Victorian era and the simplified styles of the 20th century. Balanced facades, simple roof lines, dormer windows, large front porches, and smooth brick surfaces are its characteristics. Example: 274 Broadway Street, Page 35	
Georgian, before 1860 – This style began with the British King Georges in the 18th century. These buildings have balanced facades around a central door, medium-pitched gable roofs, and small paned windows. Example: 106 Rolph Street, Page 29	
Gothic Revival, 1830-1890 – These decorative buildings have sharply-pitched gables with highly detailed vergeboards, pointed-arch window openings, and dichromatic brickwork. It is a common style in Ontario. Example: 298 Broadway Street, Page 38	
Italianate, 1850-1900 – It has wide-bracketed eaves, belvederes, wrap-around verandahs. Example: 267 Broadway Street, Page 33	

Queen Anne, 1885-1900 – This style is distinguished by an irregular outline featuring a combination of an offset tower, broad gables, projecting two-storey bays, verandahs, multi-sloped roofs, and tall, decorative chimneys. A mixture of brick and wood is common. Windows often have one large single-paned bottom sash and small panes in the upper sash. Example: 38 Ridout Street West, Page 5	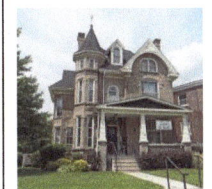
Tudor Revival – exposed timbers with stucco infill, multi-paned windows. Example: #16 – see Page 43	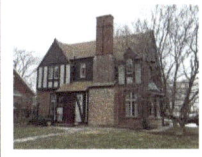

Other Books by Barbara Raue

Coins of Gold
Arrows, Indians and Love
The Life and Times of Barbara
The Cromwell Family Book
Laura Secord Discovered
Daddy Where Are You?

Montana Series
Book 1: Montana Dream
Book 2: Life on the Montana Frontier
Book 3: Montana to Boston and Back
Book 4: Montana Sons Go to War
Book 5: Montana Sons Return from War

This is a link to Barbara's website to view all of her books
http://barbararaue.ca

www.ingramcontent.com/pod-product-compliance
Lightning Source LLC
Chambersburg PA
CBHW040853180526
45159CB00001B/412